PRAISE FOR
DUBRAVKA UGRESIC

"Ugresic, a game and inquisitive critic, looks at culture from all angles, which sometimes means picking up the mic. . . . *Karaoke Culture* is an essential investigation of our times."
—*Los Angeles Times*

"Ugresic must be numbered among what Jacques Maritain called the dreamers of the true; she draws us into the dream."
—*New York Times*

"[*Karaoke Culture* is] a brilliant collection of timely essays."
—*Publishers Weekly* (starred review)

"Dubravka Ugresic is the philosopher of evil and exile, and the storyteller of many shattered lives."
—Charles Simic

"A unique tone of voice, a madcap wit and a lively sense of the absurd. Ingenious."
—Marina Warner

ALSO BY DUBRAVKA UGRESIC

EUROPE IN SEPIA

DUBRAVKA UGRESIC

TRANSLATED FROM THE CROATIAN BY DAVID WILLIAMS

OPEN LETTER

LITERARY TRANSLATIONS FROM THE UNIVERSITY OF ROCHESTER

All citations of *Envy* by Yuri Olesha are taken from Marian Schwartz's
2004 translation, published by New York Review Books.

Essays from this collection previously appeared in the following: "Fatal Attraction,"
"Liquid Times," "Jumping off the Bridge," "A Mouthful," and "Soul for Rent!" appeared
together under the title "My Own Little Mission" in *The Baffler*; "The Code," "The
Dream of Dorian Grey," "A Middle Finger," and "Who Is Timmy Monster?" appeared
together as "The Code" in *The Baffler*; "Wittgenstein's Steps" appeared as "Wittgenstein's
Steps: A Letter from Unified Europe" in *The Baffler*; an abridged version of "ON-zone"
appeared as "Out of Nation Zone" in *Salmagundi*; "Europe in Sepia" and "Mice Shadows"
appeared in *Salmagundi*; "A Croatian Fairy" appeared in *The White Review*; an abridged
version of "Can a Book Save our Life?" appeared in *Bookforum*; and an abridged version of
"Zagreb Zoo" appeared in *PEN Atlas*.

Library of Congress Cataloging-in-Publication Data: Available upon request.
ISBN-13: 978-1-934824-89-4 / ISBN-10: 1-934824-89-5

Text set in Caslon, a family of serif typefaces based on the designs of
William Caslon (1692–1766).

Design by N. J. Furl

Open Letter is the University of Rochester's nonprofit, literary translation press:
Lattimore Hall 411, Box 270082, Rochester, NY 14627

www.openletterbooks.org

CONTENTS

3. ENDANGERED SPECIES

1.

EUROPE IN SEPIA

"We are a breed of men that has reached its upper limit," he would say, *banging his mug on the marble like a hoof.*

—*Yuri Olesha,* Envy

NOSTALGIA

NEW YORK, ZUCCOTTI PARK

I visited New York in October 2011, and a couple of days after arriving, I set off for Wall Street, not having checked the exact location of Zuccotti Park. Coming out of the subway, I fortunately spotted an information kiosk.

"Excuse me, where's the, ah . . . revolution?" I asked goofily.

"Just go straight on, it's a few blocks away," replied a young guy, his face spreading into a smile. Buoyed by the smile, I got going. As the rhythm of my pulse quickened, I wondered whether a long dormant rebel virus was stirring in me. Rebel?! Well, yeah, when you line up a few historical and personal details, it's fair to say that rebellion and I are well acquainted.

My parents conceived me around the time when Tito said his famous NO to Stalin. I came into the world in 1949, when the Soviet Union and its fraternity of member states had recently accused Yugoslavia of "deviating from the path of Marxism and Leninism." The same year Tito was declared a traitor and Yugoslavia condemned to isolation. I was born on March 27. On the same date, albeit eight years previously, the slogan *Better the grave than a slave, better war than the pact*[1] was born. It was one I adopted at a tender age, and in time I developed a form of behavior, which psychologists—so adept at creating new terms—would today classify as LAT (Low Authoritarianism Tolerance) syndrome. It's entirely possible that Tito's famous NO to Stalin set me on my way as a budding naysayer. The opening line of *The Internationale*, "Arise, damned of the Earth," makes my skin tingle; *Bandiera Rossa* makes me cry. While children in other countries flicked through *The Teddy Bears' Picnic*, my picture book story of choice was about a young man named Danko.[2] Brave Danko tears his heart from his chest, lighting the way for a cowering crowd trapped in a deep, dark forest, and leads them into a sunny clearing. Danko ends up dead, of course, alone and abandoned, what else. The part where some imbecile, having just crawled out of the darkness and into the light, steps on Danko's still beating heart took root in my imagination forever. An unproductive affinity for dreamers who use their hearts as batteries has followed me unfailingly ever since.

By the time I got to grade school, together with my classmates I sent letters of support to Patrice Lumumba, imprisoned somewhere in

---

1 On March 27, 1941, demonstrations erupted in Belgrade against the signing of the Triple Pact. Demonstrators bravely took to the streets shouting slogans against Hitler and Mussolini. The slogan (in the original) *"Bolje grob nego rob, bolje rat nego pakt"* was later plucked from its historical context and engraved in the collective memory of many Yugoslavs as artfully rhyming revolutionary code.

2 The reference here is to Maxim Gorki's short story "The Old Woman Izergil."

distant Congo. As a girl I pronounced the names Jawaharlal Nehru, Gamal Abdel Nasser, Kwame Nkrumah, and Sirimavo Bandaranaike, leaders of the Non-Aligned Movement, with the same ease that today's kids pronounce Rubeus Hagrid, Albus Dumbledore, and Alastor "Mad-Eye" Moody. There's no mystery in it; I was twelve when the Non-Aligned Movement held its first conference in Belgrade. I protested against the war in Vietnam, even though I wasn't a hundred percent sure where Vietnam was. I spent my childhood sincere in the belief that everyone in the world—black, yellow, white, whatever—had the right to freedom and equality.

On the approach to Zuccotti Park I spent a moment checking my pulse. I wondered whether the slogan *Power to the workers, peasants and honest intelligentsia* hadn't done a number on me, and in this respect, whether my compatriots, those who twenty years ago accused me of being "Yugonostalgic," might have had it right after all. At the time I publically opposed the hysteria of nationalism, when I should have realized that nationalism is a matter of profit, not feeling. I opposed the war, when I should have accepted the thesis that war is just business, a way to make money by other means. My compatriots cottoned on to these things from the outset, and unperturbed, ran roughshod over the top of me, reenacting what the aforementioned imbecile from my picture book did to Danko's beating heart. Drawing near to Zuccotti Park, I wondered whether that old revolutionary fervor had been hibernating in me, lying in wait for its chance to come out, now, at the wrong time, and in a place I would have least suspected.

YUGONOSTALGIA

I found myself back in America having accepted a kind invitation from Oberlin College in Ohio, where they had organized a lecture series entitled *Remembering Communism: The Poetics and Politics of Nostalgia*. The Oberlin invitation momentarily boosted my tattered, veteran's self-confidence. It quickly atrophied. After twenty years of digging through the ruins, what more could I say about nostalgia, except from that, for me, it has long since lost its draw. The thought of getting down to work induced only fatigue. An insuperable mass of written and as-yet-unwritten texts swelled before me, my own and those of others. Then came the books, films, images, stories, memoirs, symbols and souvenirs, enough to fill an enormous store-room, a chaotic archive in which all manner of things had settled: seminal theoretical texts such as Svetlana Boym's *The Future of Nostalgia*; popular films such as Wolfgang Becker's *Goodbye Lenin*; visual art projects such as the installations of Ilya Kabakov; the heap of random exhibits that had strayed their way in there.

But who gets to play supreme arbiter and rule on an exhibit's *belonging* or *non-belonging*? The "archive" itself produces nostalgia only while it remains in chaos, while used as a storeroom, only while its existence remains "illegal." The work of postcommunist and (in the Yugoslav case) postwar artists—self-appointed archivists, "collectors of ruins," "doctors of nostalgia," "archeologists of the everyday"—only makes sense as a voluntary undertaking, and only when accompanied by the artist's recognition of the futility of his or her work. As soon as the work achieves "recognition," it immediately becomes susceptible to manipulation (although in itself worthless, nostalgia can still be a valuable commodity), and the energy that set it in motion vanishes. It is, parenthetically, in this disappearance that the fundamental paradox of any preoccupation with nostalgia resides: Nostalgia wipes its tracks, deceives its hunters, sabotages its researchers' toil, never remaining what it is or was.

The Berlin Wall fell over twenty years ago. From today's perspective it is clear that it fell in an extremely unusual manner. Instead of imploding, or simply toppling left or right, the wall crashed down from a great height, like a meteor, sending concrete dust flying everywhere. Yugoslavia collapsed two years after the fall of the Berlin Wall, like a row of dominos, toppling from the north and west toward the east and south.

At the time I exchanged an invalid Yugoslav passport for a new Croatian one. Two years later, new passport in hand, I left the country, one that had only just realized its "thousand-year dream of independence." And here's another paradox: the smaller the nation, the longer its history. Croatia declared both its independence and its (overnight) democracy, but the slogan I had adopted all those years ago—*better the grave than a slave*—was somehow triggered in me (my mistake, no doubt), and I quickly catapulted myself to Berlin.

The city had entered its fifth year of life A.W. (After the Wall). Pieces of the wall crunched beneath my feet, concrete dust particles shimmering on the backdrop of the deep blue Berlin sky, like a sea filled with billions of tiny plankton. I spent 1994 living in the old western part of the city, writing my novel *The Museum of Unconditional Surrender.* In yet another paradox, it was Berlin, not Zagreb, that served as a generator for reminiscence, as an ideal cutting desk for the montage of memories, a lens with perfect zoom and refraction, a pair of glasses custom-made for reading the Yugoslav and East European collapse.

In the immediate wake of independence, Croatian politicians and the local media (particularly the media) introduced the lilting coinage "Yugonostalgia" as a synonym for hostility toward the newly-created Croatian state. Yugonostalgics were castigated as dinosaurs in human form, people who grieved for the death of Yugoslavia. Yugoslavia, Tito, Partisans, the slogan *brotherhood and unity*, the Cyrillic alphabet, Yugoslav popular culture—all this stuff, and a lot of other stuff besides, was tossed into the "dustbin of history," into a memory zone to which admittance was strictly prohibited. Accusations of Yugonostalgia whizzed back and forth past people's heads like bullets. People erased their biographies and changed their names and places of birth, sworn atheists were baptized, restaurants scratched "Yugoslav" dishes (those believed to be Serbian) from their menus, and in school the mention of Yugoslavia in history books was reduced to a few lines. They wouldn't even give it a picture.

My Yugonostalgia had reared its head a little earlier, when Yugoslavia was still whole and there was no tangible reason to mourn its disappearance. Nostalgia is, however, a capricious beast, visiting us on a whim, turning up for no discernible reason, ambushing us at the wrong times and in the wrong places. Back then, I was haunted by an unnerving premonition that the world around me was about to suddenly vanish. This neurosis of imminent disappearance and discontinuity transformed me into an "archeologist of the Yugoslav everyday." I convinced myself that if I managed to preserve in memory the name of the first Yugoslav brand of chocolate, or the name of the first Yugoslav film (hardly a stretch, I admit), I could perhaps halt the impending terror of forgetting. When Yugoslavia finally sank, my neurosis took on a name—Yugonostalgia—and a definition: political sabotage of the new Croatian state. And I received epithets, too—traitor and Yugonostalgic. Eyewitness to how brutally and efficiently the confiscators of memory could erase collective memory and with it my personal history, I became a member of my own personal resistance movement. I defended myself by remembering—remembering as weapon of choice against the violence of forgetting. As opposed to theirs, my bullets killed no one. Mine had too short a range.

NOSTALGIA—A DOUBLE-EDGED SWORD

Back then, the Internet had yet to enter mass usage. Today, every post-Yugoslav is able to satisfy his or her Yugonostalgic appetites. There are sites with everything from old Yugoslav films, video-clips, popular TV series, pop singers, advertisements, and design concepts, to the chairs we sat in, the kitchens we cooked in, the haircuts we wore, and the fashions we followed. Today, Yugonostalgic exhibitions are in vogue. One can buy everything from souvenir socks bearing Tito's portrait and signature, to cookbooks with recipes for his favorite dishes. The theaters perform works with Yugonostalgic content; in documentaries interviewees speak freely of their Yugonostalgic impulses. Yugonostalgia, however, has lost its subversive quality, no longer a personal resistance movement but a consumer good. In the intervening time, Yugonostalgia has become a mental supermarket, a list of dead symbols, a crude memento mori stripped of emotional imagination.

Today, the bandit capitalism of transition is able to tolerate the presence of Yugoslav souvenirs in the ideological marketplace. Yugonostalgia only reinforces its position. How? Rather than being an entry point for serious research into and understanding of Yugoslav socialism, to a real and enduring settling of accounts between the old and the new, to a generator of productive memory—and possibly a better future—today's commercialized Yugonostalgia has been transformed into the opposite, into a highly-effective strategy for conciliation and forgetting. Buying a pair of souvenir Tito-socks, the post-Yugoslav symbolically lifts a twenty-year ban, removing the stigma from his or her socialist past. Here, nostalgia has radically changed in essence, no longer a protest against forgetting, a polemic with the existing system, or longing for a former life (if it ever meant that), but unreserved acceptance of the present. Put baldly, bandit capitalism can easily afford to behave like the Russian oligarch, Mikhail Prokhorov, who rented the cruiser *Aurora*, a symbol of the October Revolution, and organized a party befitting the very richest of the rich—Russian oligarchs.

On the other hand, the irritation evinced when words such as Yugo-nostalgia, Yugoslavia, Yugoslav, socialism, and communism are spoken suggests that having become Croats, Serbs, Slovenes, or whatever, citizens of the former Yugoslavia still have some way to go in freeing themselves of their Yugoslav pasts. As a result, public figures, whether politicians, writers, or artists, inevitably tag an obligatory footnote to every mention of the word Yugonostalgia. Mentioning Yugoslavia doesn't for a second mean that one mourns the country's passing, let alone that of communism—God forbid! The exhibition *Socialism and Modernity*, which opened in late 2011 at the Museum of Contemporary Art in Zagreb, both confirms and serves to inflame an irritation that has smoldered for over two decades in Croatia and other former Yugoslav republics. Visitors to the exhibition can see the first car Yugoslavia ever produced; the first Yugoslav radio and television set; excerpts from TV shows; exemplars of fashion, furniture, architecture, and design; even a trove of old bank notes, coins, posters, and photos, but the historical context remains incredibly elusive. Yugoslavia, communism, and socialism are rarely mentioned, so one is somehow left with the impression that the modernity of the fifties and the sixties was an exclusively Croatian one, one with a dissident hue, although the nature of this dissent remains ambiguous. The exhibition's curators seem afraid of the fact that Croatia was a Yugoslav republic at the time, that Yugoslav socialism brought modernity with it, and that the socialism and modernity of the time were an ideologically harmonious pair.

American capitalism uses nostalgia in a far more adroit, refined, and enticing manner. The Levi's *Go Forth* and *Go Work* campaigns are examplary of how capitalism rebrands itself and thus shores up its dominant position.[3] Deploying the aesthetics of devastated post-capitalist spaces (the abandoned workers' halls of Pittsburgh and Detroit), and using amateur rather than professional models, the images in the Levi's advertisements invoke nostalgia for erstwhile values: self-reliance, strength, honesty, work, self-respect, courage—a nostalgia for the America of the pioneers. Culled from this pioneer-America are shots of freight trains and stowaways, deserted railway tracks alongside which people trudge into an uncertain future, muscle-ripped young men bathed in sweat, scrappy bundles in hand, on their faces a visible readiness to meet life head on. Accompanying the images, phrases such as *things got broken here* absolve those to blame for the economic crisis of all responsibility, implying that the crisis is a kind of natural catastrophe that has afflicted everyone in equal measure. The bald exhortation *we need to fix it* urges people (the working class!) to spit in their palms, take matters into their own hands, and rebuild their lives—*your life is your life!* And, naturally, no one sets off to rebuild his or her life

3   Sarah Banet-Weiser offers an astute analysis of the trend in the Dutch documentary *Metamorfose van een crisis* (Aftermath of a Crisis).

bare-assed. Hence the necessity of a baseline initial investment—in a pair of Levi's.

OBERLIN, AMERICANA

Still in a daze from the change of time zone, in the morning I headed out for a walk around Oberlin. It wasn't that there was any- where to really go. My hotel looked out over a large park. On the opposite side of the park were the university buildings, and to my left the main street with a handful of shops, including the bookstore where in a few hours time I would be giving a reading. A modest poster taped to the inside of the window gave the date and time. The bookstore wasn't actually just a bookstore, but a kind of general store stocking anything and everything. Feigning effort to remain incognito, I bought a useless pair of Chinese-made slippers, a waste of both money and vanity given that the sales clerk had no idea I was the person in the poster photo. Nonetheless, it was an opportu- nity to tip my hat to my past. The store vaguely reminded me of the old Yugoslav stores of the fifties, and so in addition to the slippers I bought a copy of my book. I felt like Allison MacKenzie, who after forty years returns to Peyton Place to buy a copy of her own book, all in the hope that the hoary bookseller might recognize her.

I began my story about Yugonostalgia in the same venue later that evening, the small audience made up of students and faculty. I think my listeners were expecting me to talk about popular conceptions of Yugonostalgia, but the morning stroll around the small town center had pulled a number of mysterious threads, and suddenly images from my childhood burst into life before me. I was born and grew up in a similar small town, minus the students and the university of course. In what passed as downtown, there was an improvised cinema in what was formerly the local hotel. My mom and I would take our places on the long wooden benches (no backrests—it was the fifties!) and watch Hollywood movies. How was it that Hollywood films were my childhood entertainment? A few years after Tito's historic NO to Stalin, Yugoslav cinemas were flooded with Hollywood films, the best kind of ideological support. Even Tito was an avid cinephile, as was my mom, as was the little me.[4] *Bathing Beauty* with Esther Williams was apparently the first Hollywood film to play in postwar Yugoslav theaters.

My favorite actor was Audie Murphy, an American hero who stood barely 5' 3", and weighed only around 110 lbs., but who killed 240 Germans in the Second World War, received 33 prizes for bravery, acted in 44 films (in which he killed Indians by the score), and in the end died in a plane crash. However briefly, for us children Audie Murphy was a kind of Yugoslav Peter Pan. The world was straightforward then. Fascists were our enemies. We crushed fascists, just like the Americans, just like Audie Murphy. To be fair, Stalin crushed fascists too, but he was our sworn enemy.

Other stars soon took Audie Murphy's place: Marlon Brando, James Dean, Elvis Presley, Pat Boone, Natalie Wood, Warren Beatty . . . Mom used to subscribe to a film magazine; we'd guzzle reports of our silver screen heroes and heroines like sweet candies. Many of Mom's books were American too—*An American Tragedy* springs to mind. At high school I identified with Allison MacKenzie. She wrote poetry and went around with books clasped to her chest, as if they were some kind of protection. I carried my books like that for while, but then came other idols, other attractions . . .

---

4   Yugoslav film director Dušan Makavejev once wittily remarked that Yugoslavia's disintegration began the moment Tito opted to appoint not a sole personal movie operator, but one for each of the six Yugoslav republics.

All in all, in Oberlin's MindFair Books, it became apparent that the authentic object of my nostalgia was the America of the fifties, an America gleaned from American films shown in a small provincial theater, in a small provincial town in Nowheresville, Yugoslavia. My Yugonostalgic packet wasn't stuffed with the usual stereotypes—the red star, the hammer and sickle, the Yugoslav national anthem—all of which my young listeners perhaps expected, but with other stereotypes—Americana, Yugo-Americana. Nostalgia had betrayed me again. *Nostalgia*, you bitch . . .

I suspect my young listeners might not have completely understood my story, the names I tossed like confetti couldn't have meant much to them. Two or three of my peers in the audience nodded their heads affirmatively, recalling the early years of our mutual youth. Maybe later they wondered how it was that our childhoods had been so similar, and our countries so distant and different. I neglected to mention that I also have a little habit fed by the Internet. Whenever my mind wanders to a Hollywood star or starlet of my childhood, I immediately go to Google to tell me if he or she is still alive. Esther Williams just passed away, unfortunately. But Pat Boone is still around, thank God!

NEW YORK, WASHINGTON SQUARE

From Zuccotti Park I took a stroll to Washington Square and sat down on a bench. It was late afternoon, sultry, an Indian summer. I immediately noticed that the black guys who used to play chess were missing, as were those who hung out brownbagging it. Washington Square had long been a hangout for smokers, and now a sign at the entrance warned that smoking in the park was strictly forbidden. The scamps bumming cigarettes were gone, and with them any occasion for small talk. The park seemed distressingly well ordered, like a provincial college campus. Where were the dropouts, the refuseniks, the superfluous men and women, the alcoholics and smokers, the homeless, the pickpockets, the vagrants, the hustlers? Where were the grumblers grumbling to themselves, the idlers, the beggars, the losers, the dreamers? Where were the skeptics, the envious, the good-for-nothings, the weaklings, the humiliated and insulted, the capitulators? Where were they?

On the bench opposite me I immediately recognized a middle-aged woman. She was an actress, a film actress, until recently a poster girl for a well-known cosmetics brand. I felt a sudden compassion for the lines on her face, as if they were my own. The face of a goddess was showing the first signs of capitulation. Jesus, just think how many people walk the earth waving invisible white handkerchiefs and flags! And what about me? Where do I stand in the order of things?

One of the Zuccotti Park slogans beamed out the message: *Listen to the drumming of the 99% revolution*. For once I remembered to take photos. In those few days the Zuccotti kids were photographed so often that thirty years' worth of Japanese tourists haven't managed to take more photos of Manneken Pis, the famous little peeing boy of Brussels. And it is for this reason, this reason alone, that the drums from Zuccotti Park echoed in every corner of the globe.

From all corners, you can hear the drumming. They're sending messages to one another, the content always the same. Whether the media will end up ridiculing and destroying the kids, whether the media industry will suck them up and spit them out as profit, whether the tractable rebels will leave the confinement of Zuccotti Park and one day take to the streets to join with those from London, Barcelona, Athens, Amsterdam, Berlin, Zagreb, Moscow, and who knows where else, is, for the moment, not important. For now they're just drumming: *The days of plenty are over!*[5]

I sat on the bench, warming myself in the Indian summer sun. I let my eye wander discreetly over the actress's figure: the indistinct charcoal-colored outfit, the stooped shoulders, the body that has obviously given up worrying what a spectator might think. The actress nodded her head. I offered a friendly nod back. She didn't notice me. She had a mobile phone to her ear and was nodding to an unseen collocutor.

"What's the time?" a young guy asked. I was flustered, it had been so long since a random passerby had interrupted me with the question. Nobody asks for the time anymore. I looked at my watch. In almost all time zones watches were showing the same thing. "It's time . . . for revolution," I said. And with that I headed toward the subway.

---

5   The translated title and catchphrase of the German-Austrian film *Die fetten Jahre sind vorbei* (2004), distributed in English as *The Edukators*.

EUROPE
IN SEPIA

LATELY I'VE CAUGHT myself turning the faces and hues of Central Europe into photographs, an automatic click on an internal camera and I'm done. A second later an iPhoto program whirrs inside me: *import—effects—sepia—done.* It's as if the surrounding reality is a screen, stuck to my hand an invisible remote with three options: past, present, future. But only one of them works: past, *sepia.*

Maybe a recent sleepless night in Bratislava triggered the reflex. The hotel room had an unusual "dummy" window, facing not outward to the exterior, but inward, to the reception desk. I kept the window closed and the curtains drawn, both of which appeared to increase the density of the claustrophobia in the air. Having given up trying to fall asleep, it was probably around two in the morning when I opened the new edition of *The Economist* and stared long at a map of Europe divided into three-color zones. An alarming red color marked countries in recession, yellow the countries somehow muddling through, and green the absence of recession. Slovakia, Estonia, and Slovenia were alone in the green zone; news reports the next day announced that Slovenia had just slipped into yellow. In the hope it might send me to sleep, I browsed a tourist brochure I'd picked up at the reception. On a map of Slovakia, a settlement bearing my name northwest of Bratislava caught my eye. Rather than surprise or delight (*look, the little spot and I have the same name!*), in a flash of recognition I was overcome by the fact that ours was a kinship based on inconsequence and insignificance. Ah, that Slavic linguistic sisterhood, *dub—dubrava*, all those forests and woods, leaves and oaks, hills and valleys, water and wetlands, in Slovak all so painfully similar to my native tongue. My eye glides sullenly over the Slovak place names as if searching for lice. There's Slovensky Grob, and look, Chorvatsky Grob . . . *Grob—brijeg—grb—brlog—graba*. Grave—hill—crest—den—dike. (Shouldn't Zagreb actually be *Zagrob*, a burial place, not merely a settlement next to a humdrum hill or commonplace dike?) The margins of the brochure teem with advertisements: roast duck, goulash, gingerbread hearts, girls in national dress wearing flower wreaths in their hair . . . and then there are the bold harbingers of the new time: Thai massages, a sushi bar . . .

I wondered about my sullenness and what lay at its root. It's entirely possible that as a child I had been wound not according to Greenwich time, but rather to a socialist clock, one always rushing on ahead into the *brighter future*, toward *progress*, a tomorrow envisaged as a majestic fireworks display of a thousand shapes and colors. Maybe my childhood imagination—tattooed with the heroism of a little dog named Laika and the promise of an impending trip to the moon—permanently adrenalized the horizons of my expectations? Or had technological innovations perverted my horizons, and now, appetite unchecked, I expect the surrounding reality to behave like a 3D film, more impressive than its actual self? Isn't my sullenness the recognition that I'd set off for a place I'd categorically never set foot before, and lo and behold arrived "home"? Maybe I carry a Central European blueprint with me everywhere, and on entering the Central European zone I compare my internal sketch with the situation on the ground, my copy with the hues of my surroundings, utterly incapable of finding pleasure in the beauty of small differences. Doesn't my sullenness lie in the uncanny confrontation with my own position on the map? I mean, we all scratch where it itches most. Didn't I, preparing for the trip, toddle through the Internet and the history of Slovak literature and catch myself reading with a distinct lack of enthusiasm, the exact same way I would read the history of Croatian literature, and that consequently, among the forlorn names of Slovak writers I can easily imagine my own? Wasn't a sleepless night in a Bratislava hotel room with a dummy window facing the interior simply a painful confrontation with my own insignificance? If that's how it was, what the hell is with my "colonial" arrogance, this eruption of an almost actionable political incorrectness, my arbitrary establishing of coordinates of significance and insignificance? Why do crappy pictures of plates of goulash induce nausea and not good cheer? I'm no vegetarian. I have no call for sullenness; Slovakia is not my country, I'm here for the first time and as a guest, the hotel room with the dummy window isn't my apartment, my hosts are exceptionally gracious, goulash is a tasty dish, Bratislava a city on the Danube, and the Danube—*Dunav—Duna—Dunaj—Donau—Danube—Tuna—Dunărea*—a river with its source in the Black Forest and its mouth at the Black Sea . . .

Spanning the Danube and leading into Bratislava is what is once more (as of 2012) known as the Bridge of the Slovak National Uprising, a communist architectural hangover resembling a giant two-legged robot, its head shaped like a Pyrex dish, in which sat a rotating restaurant. Roast duck on his plate and his head in the clouds, a communist Slovak might well have felt he held the whole world in the palm of his hand. For a time, towers with rotating restaurants were ubiquitous, communist architectural chic. In the restaurant atop the TV tower on Berlin's Alexanderplatz the waitresses dress in retro-style GDR uniforms, giving their all to be as slow as they were in the good old days. Maniacal communism had maniacal architectural pretensions. Many still hold the Stalinist Seven Sisters of Moscow (and their cousins in Warsaw, Kiev, Prague, and Riga) for architectural farce, though the skyscrapers were built on American models and differ little from those in New York.

Known for a time as the "New Bridge," Bratislava's Bridge of the Slovak National Uprising lowers one down into the sleepy heart of the old town, where an affectingly Lilliputian statue of Maria Theresa on horseback greets the visitor. Like a toy stolen from a kindergarten, Maria Theresa sits opaquely in the November fog. With the faded yellows and greens of its façades, Bratislava seems half-deserted and unusually quiet, the fog like a silencer. From this side of the Danube, the bridge appears in the same fog as a grandiose futuristic promise.

We ten *intellectuals* are in town to talk of the escalation of the Euro crisis, of fear and uncertainty, of the fragile fabric of contemporary social and state structures, and of the humiliating absence of future projections. The majority of us are writers; on demand we play amateur sermonizers. The "professionals," those who really know their stuff, are in the negligible minority. Cultural managers, smalltime NGO bosses, editors of obscure magazines, university lecturers, students and volunteers—everyone is here. My "tribe." Summoned we gather, give each other a passing sniff, wag our tails, bark a little, and then we withdraw . . . until the next time. EU pennies tinkle down invisible pipes from Brussels, gratefully collected by the hands of those who call us to assembly. Only one of our number is a "star." He puts in a brief appearance, explaining to the assembled that—ecologically speaking—beef goulash has had its day: Cow dung emits way too many harmful gasses. Ecologists at least know what they're talking about when they talk about the future, or perhaps more to the point, no one doubts that they know. Seeking our devotion, our sacrifice, and our faith, ecologists are our modern prophets. When they say the end is nigh, it's believing time.

Crisis, crississ, crisssissss—the word buzzes among the old theater walls like a pesky fly. We pass down a narrow corridor, peek into the make-up room and wardrobe, stumble over dusty props, and there we are on a little stage, floodlit by antiquated spotlights and the faces of the audience. We talk, our words visibly frayed, banging into each other like heads against a wall. The air is stifling, there's a yawn in the audience, a lack of oxygen, the theater becomes cramped. We welcome the interval with relief, and in the foyer fortify ourselves with coffee. One of my tribe, a petite woman with a pretty face and prim posture is wearing children's mittens. Her hands bear a striking resemblance to plush paws. Her companion offers an explanatory footnote: "Her nightgown was synthetic, that's why she suffered so. It was remarkably fortuitous the fire didn't get her face." His voice is subdued and cold, as if he's worn out the emotional charge through overuse. The woman is a Polish émigré, a true European, dazzlingly fluent in several languages. Her prim fragile figure and paw-mittens induce a taut mixture of discomfort and sympathy. I excuse myself and search for the exit. In a second foyer sit two catatonic doormen, ghosts of communism, staring wide-eyed at a television screen. Although heady images of the demonstrations

in Zuccotti Park beam live on all international channels, they stare
transfixed at a Mexican soap. There's a bench just outside the exit
obviously intended for smokers. A Russian colleague lolls about,
puffing away like a night clerk outside a communist hotel. I join
him. At first we smoke in silence, then we chat a little about Russian oligarchs. Great guys, he says, smart, well-read, novels by
their bedsides. One bought an English daily, another a chain of
English bookstores, Russian literature's bound to make inroads into
the western market now. Yeah, what you can do, it's the law of the
jungle out there, the weakest goes to the wall. For him personally
there's no crisis, things have actually never been better. Two Slovak
girls join us, a fair relief. I notice a Central European melancholy
discreetly shading their faces like a fine foundation. Or is it just
their long eyelashes?

Central, Eastern, Southeastern Europe . . . It's a landscape I know
like the back of my hand. They were different in the time of communism; only the iconography was the same. Now it's as if the fall
of communism has felled the differences. I know how people here
breathe, the way they hide themselves, playing dead like a fox in a
fable, peasant cunning. They lower their gaze in conversation with
outsiders, practiced in the art of restrained movement, answering
every question with *I don't know*—that *I don't know* always accompanied by a wistful smile. They swallow the dumpling of betrayal
on a daily basis, fret about making ends meet, walking on tiptoes to
prevent a breach, as if expecting the dam to burst and the envisaged
flood to sweep away all in its path. They don't try planting flowers—gardening is a belief in the future, and they have no future.
Peasant fatalism and moronic sayings are all that remain for them:
A man needs a full belly and empty balls; *we've always got by, we always
will somehow.* They huddle together, withdraw into their own shells,

shrinking to their true dinky stature, only to then peddle this dinki-
ness as their chief virtue. They're hawkers of cheap souvenirs, angel
figurines everywhere, the Slovaks stealing them from the Poles,
the Czechs from the Slovaks. Croats sell gingerbread hearts and
bags of lavender. Few display any imagination—imagination doesn't
sell. They want UNESCO to protect their non-material resources;
the Croats have already hocked off *kulen* and *soparnik*.[1] Yes, they
live off souvenirs, like European Indians in a European reserva-
tion. Honey cookies, gingerbread, a bit of folklore, embroidery and
lacework, olive oil from handpicked olives, traditional local recipes.
At the markets in Vienna these Indians (Serbs? Gypsies? Macedonians?) sell fake Roman coins and fibulas. Their squaws—women
with bleached hair and faces roasted like Chinese smoked duck (sun
beds are still in fashion)—are ragpickers, traders in "original fakes,"
clothing, caps, and scarves. Everyone sells his or her bric-a-brac.
Yes, the future is definitely elsewhere. In the time of communism
watches sped ahead, now they go backwards. To bridge the time
difference, today parents herd their kids toward Singapore, Australia, Hong Kong, and Asia. No, not to Western Europe—that's
all over. Sure, after the fall of the Wall everyone perked up a bit,
breathed a sigh of relief, got comfy in their new statelets. But you
have to pay to play, so some stole, others slaughtered, and others just
enjoyed a little bum-rushing. In time their heels cooled and they
bowed their heads, as if occupied by an invisible force. Now here
they are, back where they always were . . .

"And what do you want," demurs my interlocutor, a Croat. Everyone
has always walked all over us, and yes, we bowed our heads, shut

---

1 *Kulen* is a spicy pork and red pepper sausage, *soparnik* an ancient Croatian
dish from the Poljica region of Dalmatia, a kind of chard pie dating from
before the Ottoman invasions.

our mouths, and divided into tribes. We Slavs are a sad people. We've never had, nor will we ever have, a Joyce or a Beckett. Do you know why? Because Vladimir and Estragon—that's us. We've been waiting around for centuries for someone to come, to fall from the sky, waiting's all we've ever done; we're artists when it comes to waiting. Maybe that's why, unlike others, we've never conquered or subjugated anyone. They've conquered us. Our rebellion is small beer. All we do is get drunk, smash our heads against the wall, and maybe slit our veins with broken glass from the floor. What did we inherit from the ancient Slavs? The art of breathing under water. Breathing through a reed—our authentic Slavic innovation. We've never been ambitious. Vienna, you say? We don't care about Vienna, and neither do the Slovaks. Bratislava wants to be Linz, Zagreb to be Graz or Trieste, that's the reach of our ambition. Yes, we're endangered like Indians, hence our efforts to protect what remains: language, a little mythology, a few ancient handicrafts. Our differences are small beer too: Some of us pray to the god of rain, others to the god of sun, some do their *ganga*,[2] others blow their penny whistles. We regularly summon our ghosts, excavating our ancestors' bones. We count for nothing, we don't produce anything, nor do we have the money to buy anything. We are neither producers nor consumers; no one needs us, not even our own kids.

A racing pulse—tachycardia—fatigue—nausea—anxiety—crisis. The rules of etiquette didn't prevent me fleeing Bratislava before time was called. Once home (in Croatia, in Zagreb? No, in the Netherlands, in Amsterdam!) I quickly forgot my two-day "Slovak"

---

2 *Ganga* is a dissonant form of singing—or moreover, wailing—traditional in rural Croatia and Bosnia-Herzogovina, often performed by men standing in a circle with interlocked arms.

episode. I deleted everything. Only two pictures managed to sneak into my internal album. The tiny sculpture of Maria Theresa on horseback twinkling opaquely in the November fog, and the petite woman with the beautiful face, a child's mittens drawn over tiny burnt hands. The two aren't necessarily a diptych, but both are in sepia.

Brought on by a fresh incident, here "at home" a new anxiety attack soon runs me down. Geert Wilders' party, the PVV, or Partij voor de Vrijheid, launches a website cordially inviting Dutch citizens to have their say on burning questions (*Do you have problems with recent arrivals from Central and Eastern Europe? Have you lost your job because of a Pole, Bulgarian, Romanian, or some other East European?*). The website is visited by tens of thousands of people giving vent to their resentment at the legal presence of Central, East, and Southern European immigrants. Poles, especially the Poles. Because it's the Poles who are taking their jobs. Poles steal, get drunk, they're loud and liable to criminal behavior. Poles are "human trash."

There's no reason for alarm. I'm not a Pole; for now I still pass as a Croat with a Dutch passport. The ex-Yugoslav and Bulgarian in me I'll easily hush up. I'll freeze like a fox in a fable until this storm, too, passes. I diligently pay my taxes to this water-soaked country. The damp doesn't bother me; we, we Slavs, are used to forests and trees, leaves and oaks, water and wetlands. My memes are active, they remember the old Slavic art of breathing underwater. Maybe my anxiety attack is just a tempest in a teacup. It seems that way. For now. Until some new storm rolls in. And then everything will depend on that final drop of water, and in which direction the flood surges.

WITTGENSTEIN'S STEPS

1.

Pigeons are crazy about public sculptures. For a pigeon there's no greater happiness than perching on the head of a sculpture and taking a dump. Sculptures are for people to consecrate, and pigeons to desecrate. The truth is that for some reason people are crazy about public sculptures too.

In December of last year, unidentified vandals attacked a sculpture of Marija Jurić Zagorka, a Croatian journalist and novelist. Zagorka's literary production never got its due during her lifetime, nor for many years after her death. Had it not been for the efforts of the Zagreb Center for Women's Studies—which, inter alia, had a statue erected in her honor in downtown Zagreb—her work would today be forgotten. The vandals sawed off the bronze umbrella on which the bronze authoress stood leaning in repose, the Center for Women's Studies whipped up a media frenzy, and the city fathers promptly committed to appropriating funds for a new umbrella. Appalled by the ugly incident, the next day many Zagreb residents laid old umbrellas at the statue's feet. There you go, that's canonization for you!

Croats might not be pigeons, but they still suffer a fatal attraction for public monuments. Since Croatia gained independence in 1991, many monuments to the victims of fascism have suffered damage. The majority took place in the immediate post-independence years, a time of anti-Yugoslav (anti-Serbian, and anti-communist) hysteria. The new authorities had a fair degree of empathy for vandal passions provoked by collective Croatian traumas. In historical perspective, the Croatian reaction confirmed a paradox: Trauma is sometimes greatest where there is least cause; anti-communist hysteria proved most vehement where communism itself had been most benign.

2.

The truth is, even I didn't really pay monuments any mind until I discovered a surprising truth: Most people engage in vandalism for the cash, not out of ideological or aesthetic convictions. Everyone in Holland knows who's most enamored with copper and bronze. Yes, the Poles. In February of this year statues were stolen from atop graves in the Dutch settlements of Norg and Vries. Rheden lost a statue of the writer Simon Carmiggelt, and, wary of new thefts, a statue of Queen Beatrix was spirited away into storage. A couple of years ago a public sculpture of a mother and child, erected in memory of the victims of the Second World War, was stolen from Marienberg. In 2007 a copy of Rodin's *The Thinker* was stolen in Laren. The cities of Zwolle and Nijmegen recently resolved to put their public statues in safekeeping, and in Eindhoven the police have fitted public sculptures with GPS units. If the sculptures from Eindhoven go for a stroll, the police will know where to find them.

The list of Polish sins is long: Anything with a glint of copper is a target for Polish thieves. If the trains aren't running, it's because the Poles have ripped out the copper cables. If there's a power loss, it's because the Poles have pilfered the copper cables from a few wind-mills, the pride of the Dutch national landscape. If a remnant from the First World War explodes in the Ypres region, it's because the Poles (ah, those moles!) have been burrowing the fields in search of copper, happy to accept the risks. The Dutch—for whom the Ger-mans, who thieved Dutch bicycles at the close of the Second World War, had long been the preferred enemy—now blame the Poles for everything. In the settlement of Menaldum the police seized the bicycles of Polish workers living at the Schatzenburg trailer park, convinced they were stolen. It turned out the bikes had been given to the Poles by their employer so they'd be able to ride to work. "Poles" (a collective term for all East Europeans, of whom Poles are simply the most numerous) most often live in what the Dutch refer to as "Polish hotels," which in reality means in cabins or camp trailers on the peripheries of the burgs where they work. The Dutch rent camp trailers to Poles for between fifty and eighty euro a week. That's why many Poles prefer to sleep in tents. "Poles like working in Dutch horticulture. How can I best explain it? It's a matter of chemistry. Dutch growers and Poles are like peas in a pod." That's how Johan de Jong, the avuncular general director of Holland Con-tracting, explained things to the media. He's just one of the many Dutch who help Poles earn a wage in Holland, the average wage for undocumented labor being about four euro an hour, and it goes without saying that most Polish labor is indeed such.

There's a legend about how a couple of Dutch discovered copper wire while fighting over who had dibs on a copper coin they'd spotted in the street. The Poles have now got themselves mixed up in the story. In almost every country the greatest thefts are perpetrated by *natives*—in Holland, the Dutch; in Croatia, the Croats; in Poland, the Poles—snugly protected by myths of great theft and devastation being the work of *others*, chiefly *foreigners*. Sometimes that *other* is a Gypsy, sometimes a Jew, other times it's a Pole, Romanian, Serb, or Albanian. There's no voice of reason that might prevent an embittered Dutchman from accusing a Pole of thieving cabbages from his garden. That's just how things are for the moment.

Poles don't steal cabbages. Poles steal bronze and copper. Not even Slovaks steal cabbage. Slovaks steal teeth. In a video clip he filmed himself and uploaded to the Internet, a Slovak recently admitted that he'd long been burgling the graves of famous people buried at the Zentralfriedhof, Vienna's central graveyard. The teeth-stealing Slovak initially made off with the watches of the deceased, but soon figured he might earn more on celebrity teeth. Apart from those of Johann Strauss and Johannes Brahms, who forensics experts have confirmed are missing teeth, the Slovak claims to be hoarding the teeth of many other famous dead, prompting the Viennese police to open the graves of Beethoven, Schubert, Schönberg, and others, just to check if all bones are present and accounted for. Charges are pending against the unusual Slovak with a fetish for pillaging celebrity skeletons' teeth.

3.

I went to Ireland in June of this year. A Dublin friend and I set off by car for Doolin, and from there took a small boat to Inisheer, the smallest of the three Aran Islands. Lashed by a stormy silver sea and menaced by a sky of black-gray clouds, Inisheer was a place of dramatic desolation. In a local café—the house of one of the island-ers—you could buy hand-knitted scarves and caps, grab a coffee from the vending machine, and try a piece of local apple strudel, all of which we dutifully did. From the tight-lipped proprietress, who never set down her knitting needles, we learned there was a doctor on the island, a Croat from Zadar. Making our way down the road to the ferry terminal we came across a lonely figure, a man pushing two bicycles, wearing a suit splattered in white paint, on his nose a huge pair of glasses with yellowed lenses. The glasses could have been those of a con man, a motorcyclist, or a scuba diver, but who would know.

"Excuse me, do you live here?"

"Aaaa . . ."

An indiscernible sound emerged from the man's mouth.

"And might you know where the local doctor lives?"

"Aaaa . . ." he pointed off into the distance.

"You're not Irish?"

"Iiii . . . Latvian . . ." he said, his mouth spreading into a tooth-less grin.

Our interlocutor had a dark-red complexion, as islanders in the north seas often do, bloodshot from constant exposure to the assaults of the wind, almost as if perma-tanned—but inside out. He was, I think, blind drunk.

Like our lonely Latvian on Inisheer, at least two-hundred-thousand Poles and other East European immigrants have made their way to and through Ireland in recent years, and it's fair to say that the Irish love affair with "Easterners" is over. Unemployment is soaring, and demands that "Poles" be banned from residing in the country for more than two years are becoming increasingly shrill.

4.

In Dublin I set off for the National Botanic Gardens, where even die-hard Dubliners are thin on the ground. Home to over seventeen thousand plant species from around the globe, the gardens were founded at the end of the eighteenth century by the Royal Dublin Society. Biodiversity is the gardens' ideological plume and pride. My attention was drawn to plaques mounted next to certain plants, emblazoned with the question *Why is it a problem in Ireland?* and an explanation of said problem in somewhat smaller type. These eye-catching "wanted posters" taught me a lot: for example, that the South American *Gunnera tinctoria*, which grows to a height of two meters, is particularly invasive. Wherever *Gunnera tinctoria* takes root, native flora just doesn't stand a chance, and consequently this ambitious plant is soon to be banned. The same applies to the giant rhubarb, and this is entirely understandable; a fleeting glance at its mighty leaves is enough to sow fear. *Sasa palmata*, a wide-leafed Japanese bamboo that grows to three meters, is likewise a threat to native flora; native sons are strangled dead wherever this particular Japanese immigrant takes root. The impressively named *Rhododendron × superponticum* is a hybrid that gladly leaps garden fences, integration and adjustment an absolute breeze. But rumor has it that it sabotages the regeneration of native trees and so it too is threatened with permanent expulsion from Ireland. The Asian *Rosa rugosa*, a pretty rose-colored shrub that grows on sand dunes alongside the ocean and speeds the erosion of native sands, is best described as a kind of floral Trojan horse. And so its time has also been called; every further contact with Irish soil is to be officially banned. *Crassula helmsii*, an aquatic invader that launched its invasion of Ireland from far-off New Zealand, is particularly noxious; resistant to frost, once it takes root it's impossible to dig out.

Some species propagate so quickly that they've changed the face of the Irish landscape. A worried taxi driver treated me to a passionate tirade against floral immigrants, singling out the cordyline palm, which in New Zealand goes by the rather unromantic name of cabbage tree. "Ireland never looked like this!" he moaned. "It's all because of those damn palms!" And, it's true, some parts of Ireland, particularly at dusk, look like suburbs of Los Angeles.

Quite parenthetically, in Dublin I was a guest at a literary festival, which had nothing to do with my native soil, with the former Yugoslavia, present-day Croatia, or the Balkans. The moderator at my event, an affable fellow, confessed to me that he had no connection with what I was to talk about either, but that the organizers had asked him to be involved when they found out his long-deceased mother was a product of Croatian *terroir*. Who knows, perhaps the organizers had visited Croatia at some point and it'd seemed to them that Croats could only manage alongside other Croats, and perhaps they'd simply thought I'd feel more at ease with an Irishman whose mother was a Croat than an Irishman whose mother was an Irishwoman or who-knows-what. I felt a bit like a cabbage they'd intercepted at the border without a botanical visa, but I certainly didn't hold it against the fine people of Dublin. Dublin—a city that has named its two imposing bridges after writers, one after Beckett, the other after Joyce—won my heart forever. The Croatian mother thing could've happened anywhere, because as far as *that thing* is concerned, it's just how most Europeans are. Yes, Europe is organized like the National Botanic Gardens in Dublin; everyone wears a plaque bearing his details around his neck—point of origin, level of invasiveness, and threat posed to native specimens all clearly documented.

But what has all this got to do with Wittgenstein? The National Botanic Gardens are also home to a glasshouse full of tropical plants, which you enter down three steps. Ludwig Wittgenstein spent the winter months of 1948–49 in Dublin. A bronze plaque mounted on one of the steps claims that Wittgenstein liked to sit on the steps and write. I sat down and let my mind wander. What did I think about? Nothing very scientific. About how Europe in its entirety is irreparably tribal, how practiced it is in the art of world wars, and how this makes a new one a constant possibility. This time because of a "Pole"; because of that Latvian on Inisheer; because of a Serb or a Croat, both practiced in desecrating each other's headstones; because of that Slovak who steals teeth from skeletons; or for some other reason—for the usual reason, money. Then the thought occurred to me that Wittgenstein might well have been sitting on these steps at the very moment my mother gave birth to me. And then, having severed the umbilical cord, I asked myself what in my life—a chaotic hold in which a socialist childhood, the disintegration of Yugoslavia, civil war, new passports and fractured identities, betrayals, exile, and a new life in a West European country all mix and mingle—what in my lifetime had actually been realized of all the things promised to us by communist ideologues, Hollywood films, the dapper ideologues of consumerism, the homespun ideologues of nationalism, the ideologues of European unification, by gurus of every stripe and shade?

The question bore into me like a poisonous thorn, my heart began to pound and I was overcome with fear, a sudden fear of the empty screen, of the absence of future projections . . . So what, said a consoling internal voice, why do we need future projections—in the near future we're to live much longer, at least on average (who still wants to live longer in a world like ours?!); and we're sure to live better (no one's promising that anymore!); and even if we don't live better, we're definitely going to live in greater freedom (yeah right!), in a world without borders (pull the other one!); in a world of solidarity and justice (enough already!); in a world of solidarity and justice we're going to live like slaves: like s-l-a-v-e-s (hey now, hey now!); don't get hung up on the details, *but always take flight to where there is a free view over the whole single great problem, even if this view is still not a clear one.* Wittgenstein, old boy, you're bleating, it's the only thing you know how to do. I'm not bleating, I just know that *a man will be imprisoned in a room with a door that's unlocked and opens inwards, as long as it does not occur to him to pull rather than push . . .*

And amazingly, following Wittgenstein's instructions, my terrified thoughts pried opened the door, fluttered their way outside and raced off toward the Asiatic steppes; my thoughts deftly leapt the frothy crests of waves on the Indian Ocean, soaring above the snowy Nepalese peaks: My thoughts skated the slipstream down onto the plains, slinking through the grass like tigers; God, there was almost nothing my hyper-mobile thoughts, my sensuous thoughts, my thoughts, seductive like a *National Geographic* clip, couldn't manage. There, on Wittgenstein's steps, I calmed my racing pulse, *ssshhh*, and renounced the prognosis I'd just offered: Bury those fears, forget that nonsense, it's just these damn gardens. I'd completely forgotten. I was in the stifling heat of the tropics.

MICE
SHADOWS

YES, INDEED, TIME and space, the ends of the earth, and all manner of things besides, can in a given moment become muddled, inducing a jagged sense of internal terror. For months we're oblivious and inured, then our fingernail catches a chance thread, and pulling on it, reality, like a woolen jumper, unravels before our eyes. Sometimes it's a noise that gets to us; the disarming crash of a dropped glass, the shattering of a porcelain cup ringing out like a child's scream, the creaking of wormholes in the night, the barely audible patter of mouse paws. Sometimes it's the routine but unforeseeable situation that unsettles us; a delayed flight, a tedious hold-up in traffic, a gaze caught unaware . . .

Who knows what pulled the thread this time? Was it the half-opened door leading from the reception of the Hotel Flanders into an adjoining room, where the melancholic face of Romy Schneider gazed out from a poster for an October 2012 film retrospective, or was it the two receptionists, little goggle-eyed gray mice, Romy's triste counterpoints?

In late November 2012, I stood at the entrance to the Hotel Flanders in Ghent, waiting for the taxi the youthful receptionist had called for me. It was morning, the city blanketed in a fog that looked like it had every intention of hanging around until spring. Shaded by a low and murky sky, the façades of nearby buildings appeared in worse repair than they actually were. Somewhere on my left I sensed a tram I glimpsed yesterday slip by, swiftly as a blind woman, the name of its terminal station—MOSCOU—on the front. It's entirely possible that this Moscow (yes, tram number four!), hurtling through the fog, was but a morning apparition. Yet the vertical letters to my left—SAIGON—they were no apparition; at any moment it seemed they might slide from the building's façade and crash down onto the footpath below. Was it this moment of hostage in the fog between "Moscow" and "Saigon" that tripped the switch of my internal anxiety? Or was it yesterday's failed attempt to pry a Ghent–Amsterdam train schedule out of the two receptionists, the pair of goggle-eyed gray mice? Online train timetables were apparently a new thing for them, and even when in a moment of final desperation I asked them to try the Deutsche Bahn site, they managed to google Deutsche Bank. Piped jazz screeched in from somewhere, and behind their mousey faces flickered the melancholic and all-empathetic smile of Romy Schneider.

Or perhaps the thread was pulled by the young conference organizer, who couldn't give me the name of Belgium's reigning monarch (at the time it was Albert II), soft-soaping me with the line that he wasn't interested in European royal houses—a lame excuse for a young Anglicist specializing in Victorian literature. But on the subject of Belgium, personally he feels more German than Belgian, which naturally makes his ignorance of the Belgian monarchy all the more understandable. I look at him, hair cropped short,

cleanly-shaven, hipster glasses, the chic suit and vest, the kind
of polished black shoes worn to weddings and funerals—the *nerd*
look is obviously his schtick. Above his head, like a saintly aura, an
imagined PowerPoint fires up, scenes from his future professional
success assembling: marriage, two children, a wife—preferably Japanese, thin as a twig—research projects, his name a toboggan run for
donor money, students just like him, slimers and asskissers, ever at
the ready to laugh at his every dorky joke. My gaze can't get anywhere near his pupils. He didn't have a handle on the King of Belgium, but he knows all about the cost of train tickets. He'll get me
the cheapest fare, one that will see me travel five hours from Ghent
to Amsterdam instead of the regular two. My turn at the conference
is as an unpaid keynote speaker. I'm not under the protective skirt
of a university, there's no professorly pension waiting for me, I'm of
no use as a referee for this or that scholarship, this or that job—why
shouldn't he save forty euro and have me travel five hours instead
of two? This is his moment. Isn't *Your time is now!* the slogan for
a brand of men's luxury watches? The Twitter-bird perches on the
conference program, he's to thank for that: Yes, you can now follow a scholarly conference on the reconfiguration of authorship on
Twitter. Around him other young Anglicists blather on about new
phenomena: twitterature, SMS-novels, collective writing, collaborative authorship, constructions of authorship, fan fiction. Again I try
to connect with his pupils. My young "executor" (oh yes, the author
and authorship need to be fundamentally reconfigured!) hides
behind his glasses, replacing the absence of eye contact with a smile
reconfiguring his surroundings. Smiley face!

But maybe the thread was pulled by Eefje, another vernal Anglicist
who joined an esteemed elderly professor and me for coffee during
the break. Eefje didn't know who I was, and didn't care to; it was

the venerable professor she wanted to talk to, whom she was out to
impress.

"The creative period in every writer's life is limited," she said.

"What do you mean by that?" the elderly professor inquired.

"Roth should have quit ages ago! He left his *I'm done* way too
late. Salman Rushdie's finished, Martin Amis washed up, Margaret
Atwood too, all of them, and heaps of others besides, they're like
the living dead!" Eefje wielded her invisible sword through the air.

"And what are your plans?" asked the elderly professor.

"I've just finished my first novel," said Eefje briskly, vivaciously
flicking her fabulous curls.

Perhaps the thread was pulled by what I saw on the train from
Antwerp to Ghent, faces like they'd escaped from old oil paintings,
having first changed their hairdos and clothes; faces with defects,
a little deformed, mouths too big, eyes too small, jaws a little too
heavyset, faces too cramped, or too long, bodies too short . . .
Grayed faces, out-of-time, just like the landscape through which the
train journeyed, one a passenger would swear was more Hungarian
or Romanian than Belgian. And then there was the time itself, as
if we'd left the present, as if it were the fifties or sixties—see that
young woman on the platform, the tailored green hues of her coat, a
belt accentuating her slim figure, the high heels, blood-red painted
lips. The woman looks freezing and soaked to the skin, but she's
not; she gets up on her tippy-toes and passionately kisses a man
who is shaved bald and otherwise utterly nondescript. The passion is
from some other time, not from the present, the scene seems unreal,
as if staged for a black-and-white shoot for a street fashion magazine: She's a beauty (though she shines only today; tomorrow she'll
too have grayed, shriveled like a potato), he a pimp. The train rolls
on through fields that sink into a wispy fog. Here and there horses

stand motionlessly in the whiteness, as if under a spell. At every station I ask myself why Belgians enter the train and so resolutely sit themselves on the empty seat beside you, never inquiring whether it's free. An older gentleman lowers his skinny butt onto the seat next to mine as it were a bag, though the seat opposite me is free, the seats diagonally across likewise . . .

Or perhaps the unraveling began a few days before I sat in the Ghent-bound train, when at Schiphol Airport, waiting for a flight to Vienna, I entered an airport bookstore, desperation etched on my face, and bought a third copy of Julian Barnes's *The Sense of an Ending*. The first time it was because I was curious, the second and now third time simply to suppress any urge to buy *Fifty Shades of Grey*. I grumbled to myself about the market's restrictiveness, its lack of imagination, how besides two books—*Fifty Shades of Grey* on the one hand, and *The Sense of an Ending* on the other—airport bookstores don't have anything else I might buy. The latter carries the symbolic imprimatur of literary quality, the former a passing literary brouhaha. Waiting for my flight I watched a girl opposite me, who, truth be told, was no different than the girl sitting next to her, or the young guy leaning up against the wall, or the guy sitting next to me, or the guy who had taken off his shoes and stretched himself out on a leather airport armchair, playing with his iPhone. They were all fiddling with their iPhones. I'm ready to bet that the more serious and sullen their faces, the more banal the content on the little screen captivating their attention. The girl sitting across from me rhythmically stroked her long, polished fingernails up and down the smooth surface of her mobile phone, as if arousing her clitoris. Was that what the faintly pornographic smirk on her face gave away? With an expression suggesting exhaustion, she then packed her mobile phone in her handbag and took out a little round mirror, beginning a thorough examination of her teeth, intermittently using the blood-red nail of her right pinky finger as a toothpick.

Or perhaps the unraveling started a couple of weeks before, kicked off by the girl with the sweet round face (one that could have just as easily been a boy's), short boyish haircut, unmarked skin, her narrow eyes grated by silvery eyelashes. She too had that out-of-time look, an impression accented by the shape of her eyes, which drooped softly at the corners. Unflattering light might have easily transformed her into an old woman. I didn't need a guide, chaperone (I was only going to be there twenty-four hours), or translator (her English was an incomprehensible shriek in any case); it was she who needed me. As she explained, she was studying philosophy and literary criticism, working the literary festival was a good way to earn a little on the side. Inter alia, she'd been assigned to me to discreetly suggest a hierarchy, one of which she was naturally oblivious.

The festival organizers never showed their faces; we writers and our local fixers—my young student among them—fronted the media and festival public. The expectation was that we were to praise the organization of the festival (which I dutifully did); to express our delight that the festival had given us the opportunity to hang out for a bit in an unexpectedly charming city (our cultural tourism merrily financed by the EU); to express our joy at the chance to mix and mingle with other writers and chat about important literary matters (an absolute whopper—at literary festivals writers avoid each other like the plague). Several interviews later I told the girl, who was patiently playing wallflower, that I was going to head off and find something to eat. She kindly offered to accompany me, and a few minutes later we were seated in a restaurant. The girl, who to that point had been like a mouse peeking out from a sack of grain, quickly livened up and ordered a meal in a self-assured voice, as if she were intending to pay for it. I paid, for myself and for her. And it was then I noticed a detail that shook me to the core. It was hard not to notice, because the girl didn't make any real effort to conceal it. Her nimble fingers spirited the bill from the saucer and discretely slipped it in her handbag, all the while staring blankly at me through the quaint verticals of her eyelashes. There was really nothing there, no apology, no unease, nothing at all, and this, I guess, was what winded me. I don't even know how to explain why it hurt so much. The girl had obviously received some kind of allowance from the festival organizers (*take her out to lunch if that's what she wants, just keep the bill*). She'd squirreled a little tip away for herself, no big deal, just the crumbs from the table. It was a mouse's theft, and in any case, there was a kind of justice in it all. In her eyes, I belong to the "upper class." I could have explained to her that at these kinds of events I feel like an itinerant actress on a fairground circuit, performing my routine for a hot meal, and, if fortune smiles, a coin or two—but the girl wouldn't have believed me. I belonged to a different social orbit, between us an irreconcilable gulf. She took what was hers; she didn't need my or the organizers' blessing, her conscience was clean. And in her, in a moment of premonition, I caught a glimpse of a potential "executor." The image scurried past me like a mouse's thin shadow. Yes, one day she'll be sitting in a publishing house somewhere, deciding whether to acquire my book, or she'll work at a newspaper, if there are still newspapers, and ever so sure of herself pass judgment on my work (didn't she say she was studying literary criticism?). The girl looked at me with her vacant stare, and I asked myself how it was I hadn't noticed it before, the mouse's shadow. Look, how many there are, everywhere . . .

At the airport, waiting to go home after my twenty-four-hour jaunt, I watched a young airport worker inadvertently inspire a group of female travelers to put on an unusual show. The women were lit up like Christmas trees, adorned with garish earrings, necklaces, and rings. The young guy asked each of them to remove their jewelry, place it on a plastic tray, and send it through the scanner. The first woman obediently removed hers, but the second—having figured the whole process was going to drag—decided to have few laughs along the way, and took her jewelry off as if performing a striptease. The kid went as red as a peasant bride. Some of the other women proved more imaginative still, one opening her mouth and pointing to a gold crown, gesturing to the kid to see if she should take that off too. Their infectious bonhomie sprayed the airport like frothy beer. From one of them I learned that they were all old friends, that they were from Israel, and that they'd come to have a look around "the country of their forebears," which, by and large, meant visiting ashes sprinkled through Auschwitz, Majdanek, Treblinka . . .

I waited in front of the Hotel Flanders as if hypnotized, not knowing how long I'd been waiting—five, ten, twenty minutes? I remembered a visit to Moscow (Moscou!) thirty years before and the feeling of "hunting a taxi" (*ohota na taksi*), the moments of sheer panic when a taxi seemed the last refuge, the only salvation from the threatening cold of Moscow's public spaces; from a square or street preparing to swallow us up; from a desperate sense of there being no escape; from the turbid ugliness of the urban landscape, when a taxi seemed the only remaining beacon of hope . . .

"No, this can't be!" I mumbled, looked at my watch, and returned to the reception. The receptionist's youthful face peered out from behind the counter: A tuft of hair raised on his forehead like a little horn, high fine cheekbones, a pointy nose, that same gray hue . . .

"Are you sure you called a taxi?" I asked, catching my breath.

He gave a start and opened his mouth to reply, but at that moment a taxi pulled up in front of the hotel and I, completely forgetting him, hurtled off toward it.

"To the station!" I cried breathlessly. Sitting down, I felt the accumulated tension in me clear like a fog. I just need to get to the station as soon as possible, just to take a seat in the train, I thought. The taxi driver was a Turk from Konya. He'd been here for four years. He likes it, he'll stay, of course he's going to stay, he hasn't the slightest intention of going anywhere else, or, heaven forbid, going back . . .

THE CROATIAN FAIRY

A fairy with a tricolor flag emerged from the sea before them, declaring: "Croats! You are few, and yet you want the most beautiful country in the world! I'm here to help. You shall have many enemies and shall wage war many times for this country. This is why your flag is red. Red from the blood you shall spill to defend her. And white is your flag too. So white and pure must your souls remain. Be truthful. Do not hate. Believe in one God!" That's what the fairy said to our ancestors. And instead of the deep blue sea, she submerged into the blue of the Croatian flag.

(Dinka Juričić, "The Croatian Fairy," Happy Steps 4: Croatian Language Primer for Fourth Grade, *2011)*

1.

This is how our story begins. Apparently it happened sometime in mid-November 2012. But I was after the exact date. I printed off ten newspaper reports, but to no avail. Useless temporal references such as "three days ago," "two days ago," "for days now," "on Friday," left the reader to do the math. I couldn't stop myself hammering "*When* was the brutal rape in Podstrana?" into Google. But only got reports headed "*What* happened in Podstrana?"

Podstrana is a place in Croatia near Split, on the road to Omiš, one of those sprawling settlements along the coast where begining and end are unclear. The unrendered façades are the defining feature of

the many half-finished houses; residents of the sprawl are unperturbed by raw concrete block. Like many other coastal settlements,
Podstrana is a joint criminal enterprise of humankind against sea
and shore, one that will naturally go unpunished; firstly, because the
crime is communal, and secondly, because communal consciousness
of it doesn't exist. Some students had a party in one such house sans
façade, drinking three bottles of whisky and a bottle of mead. One
of the girls was admitted to Split Hospital at 6:30 P.M., where doctors spent four hours fighting for her life. The papers first reported
that the twenty-year-old had been raped with a broken beer bottle,
then that it had been a blender, and finally, that she'd been raped
by the hand of Roko Šimac, an otherwise model student—as his
father told the papers. The doctors said they'd never seen anything
like it in their lives; internal organs completely massacred, gaping
wounds to the vagina and intestine, wounds that could have only
been inflicted by the violence of a human hand. The girl is recover-
ing in Split Hospital, and doesn't remember anything. Doctors will
need to perform several more operations. Roko Šimac is being held
for questioning; he can't remember anything either. The remaining
partygoers have been released. Apparently they left Roko and the
girl in the living room to make love. Some went into another room
to play computer games, others out into the yard. They said they
didn't hear any screaming, and had there been any, they wouldn't
have heard it because the music had been up so loud. Before the
party, Roko Šimac had posted a picture on his Facebook profile, of
himself and a girl (presumably not the one he raped), his attendant
comment: *Why sweep her off her feet when a smack will do the trick?*

2.

My frantic reaction to the missing date is defensive; a reaction
against the madness of the surrounding reality, a helpless attempt

to bring it to heel. Soon I am to head south, first for a brief stay in Budapest, then on to Zagreb. As my entry into a different time zone grows imminent, panic has taken hold.

In Zagreb it's as if all clocks stop. Maybe the problem is with me, imagining things that aren't there, maybe the geography bears no relation to my sense of temporal numbness. In any case, the more clocks there are, the more our sense of time dissipates. The media fabricates events rapid-fire, according each equal value, after all, news is news: a girl brutalized, a parliamentary session, a corruption scandal, tits and ass—just repeat in a different order: a parliamentary session, tits and ass, a corruption scandal, a girl brutalized. At some point reality itself gets caught in the tumble, as if competing with the media, and we, bowed and battered consumers, sell the media devil our souls at cut rates. He lures and enchants them, like a cat toying with a half-dead mouse. Technological innovations are syringes of temporal adrenalin, fueling the sense that time is surging irreducibly ahead. Once we killed time chin-wagging over coffee, today we kill it texting and tweeting. Gossip is the last form of concern for our fellow man—that's how one journalistic wit put it. Perhaps it's our final and only form, which explains our jostling as we wade the oceans of digital gossip. From screens and displays, from smartphones large and small, the human soul flashes a cheesy grin.

3.

In mid-November 2012, the beloved face of Croatian general Ante Gotovina beamed from Croatian TV screens, front pages, and posters. Tens of thousands gathered in Split on November 16 to celebrate his release (along with that of the relatively media-friendless Mladen Markač) from a prison at the Hague war crimes tribunal, his touching down on homeland soil. The same day a hundred thousand gathered in Zagreb's main square. There were prayers, tears of joy, candles, streamers and firecrackers, singing, hugs and embraces—a spectacular display of collective (male!) national hysteria. The two generals had been exonerated of their roles in a "joint criminal enterprise" to ethnically cleanse some 250,000 Serbs from Croatia during a 1995 offensive code-named Operation Storm. Many Serb houses were burned to the ground (20,000 the best estimate), Serb property ransacked and looted, and around 600 Serb civilians murdered. Pressure from the international community initiated a restitution process that never got off the ground. It was thus that the dream of Franjo Tuđman, "the father of the Croatian nation," came true. The number of Serbs in Croatian has shrunk from 12 percent before the war to 4.36 percent in 2011. The mass sackings, harassment, expulsions, the extorting of their houses and apartments, the discrimination and terror—all of this and a lot more besides—began before the war itself, and long before their "humane" and "voluntary" resettlement. (No one, of course, will ever acknowledge this, and even if they did, and it turned out to be true, it happened twenty years ago—so who cares.) The columns of Serb refugees, American ambassador Peter Galbraith sitting briefly in solidarity with them on a horse-drawn cart, were captured and broadcast on global television.

The acquittal of the two Croatian generals, particularly that of Ante Gotovina, a figure pregnant with symbolism, closes the file on what Croats call the Homeland War, absolving the homeland of any lingering guilt, declaring it an innocent and brave victim, wiping clean every stain from its defensive war, and returning, for a moment, the shattered honour of a long roll of murderers, looters, arsonists, and thieves. The Hague verdict triggered a long pent-up national orgasm. Like Franjo Tuđman, who was fond of a pigeon or two, Gotovina released birds of peace, appealing to Croats to look to the future, calling to the "self-exiled" Serbs to return, and, in light of his acquittal, again affirming that his testimony to the Hague judges had been beyond reproach: "I live with a sense of satisfaction that my actions were those of an honest and dedicated military officer who gave his all in difficult circumstances."

4.

Who is this Gotovina fellow? It depends on your sources. Glancing at the Ante Gotovina Foundation's website, you won't find much more than a handful of bank accounts soliticing donations. All these years the Foundation has been "fighting for the truth," meaning Gotovina's release. His wife, also a member of the Croatian armed forces, heads the Foundation. For the most part, the Croatian Wikipedia entry confines itself to Gotovina's military role in the Homeland War. Other sites offer more eye-opening biographical details: that at sixteen Gotovina ditched school, and at seventeen made his way to France, where he joined the Foreign Legion. Having trained as a paratrooper, he served his unproblematic duty in problematic African countries. He then worked as a bodyguard, Jean-Marie Le Pen one of his clients. Sentenced to jail for a number of criminal activities, he fled first to Argentina, and then to Guatemala, where he trained right-wing paramilitary groups. Arrested on his return to France, he served but the briefest of sentences. He arrived back in Croatia in 1991, and soon rose to the highest military rank. Ten years later he was indicted by the Hague tribunal for war crimes committed during Operation Storm and, until his spectacular arrest in the Canary Islands in 2005, spent several years on the run. After seven years in pre-trial detention, Gotovina was acquitted on appeal, surprising many observers. A few months prior the Hague court had found him guilty and sentenced him to twenty-four years jail.

Ante Gotovina is a fairy tale about Croatian success. Many of the half-million Croatian veterans identify with Gotovina; he's one of the guys. His is a story about a poor kid from a Catholic family, who flunks school, heads out into the big wide world, where, yeah, he gets up to a bit of mischief, but as a professional murderer in wartime and bodyguard in peacetime, he masters lucrative dark arts. The homeland imperiled, Gotovina made haste in returning to defend it. Today, happily married for the third time, he owns an imposing villa in Pakoštane, built by his friends, acolytes, and brothers-in-arms while he was behind bars. The local municipality made its own contribution to Gotovina's familial bliss, gifting its favorite son the land, which sits in a pine forest on a quiet inlet fifty meters from the sea, adjoining the once prosperous Club Med complex where, according to an empathetic journalist, young Ante first acquired a taste for French culture. How much has this Croatian fairytale cost the Croatian taxpayer? No one knows; the figures are one of Croatia's most closely guarded state secrets. A villa in Pakoštane is chump change, a little gift that keeps on giving. In any case, who's ever heard of a national hero having to buy his own lunch? On the subject of lunch, local residents slaughtered a fattened calf and organized a folksy reception in his honor.

5.

For my young niece, no dots connect Homeland and Gotovina. The only thing she's worried about is *when's this Gotovina guy gonna go away!* This Gotovina guy is hogging every channel, and she can't watch her cartoons. Her saying *when's this Gotovina guy gonna go away!* simply means *when can I watch* Tom and Jerry *again?*

Yet in December, the two of us will together go over school stuff about Nature and Society. The final mid-year class is about the Homeland. We have to revise all its symbols, learn the national anthem and the like. For her benefit I try paying closer attention to the Croatian coat-of-arms. I wonder what a military ordinariate is, what this imposing new structure in Zagreb, a monster from Albert Speer's archive of unrealized projects, actually does. The papers say that the Military Ordinariate, the construction of which was financed directly from the state budget, is now seeking new funds for a bigger cathedral. And meanwhile, four hundred thousand people are unemployed, another hundred thousand are employed but not being paid, almost thirty percent of the country's four million citizens are on a pension, a half million of them pensioned veterans of the Homeland War. Half a million! A Dad's Army of this size would make a country far bigger than Croatia tremble in fear. If we've got half a million retired on pensions, how many have we got on active duty? The Republic of Croatia's armed forces are a complex beast, with so many different units it's hard to keep track. And that's not counting the legions of police. Like all military ordinariates, ours is a legitimate child parented by the Holy See and the Croatian church, an institution for the pastoral and spiritual care of men and women in uniform, soldiers and police. A military ordinariate is a kind of spiritual beauty salon, an institute for the Catholicization of the armed forces and the police, a work of alchemy—that of turning shit into gold. It works in Croatia, a country of small-time grifters. Priests are alchemists too, which just goes to show that everything is in its place.

6.

My acquaintance Piroška knows well the effect she has on people—men, women, girls, boys. A friend designs Piroška's clothes, a modiste trying to infect Budapest with Lolita-style. Piroška is already thirty-something, but her striking, sleek figure and baby face work to her advantage. People are drawn to her the second they lay eyes on her, and it's usually some time before they take their leave. The way she dresses, all those miniskirts, petticoats, the taut waist, ribbons in her hair, her bangs, buttons, and clownish pins, all make propinquity a must. People huddle around stroking her hair, ribbons, and bows. There's nothing erotic in any of this, and Piroška knows that. She patiently grins and bears it all.

"People are weirdoes," she says merrily. "We're all weirdoes . . ."

Every time Piroška gets ready to go out, I imagine an army of dwarves and dwarfettes attending to her, combing and braiding, weaving multicolored ribbons in her hair, ironing her petticoats, corseting her up, zipping, buttoning, and unbuttoning . . . My little niece would give any thing to have Piroška for an aunt. She'd trade me and her whole collection of Barbies for a single Piroška.

I saw Piroška at a Budapest literary festival in late November, the venue a boat docked on the banks of the Danube. Festival guests had already dispersed by the time some ten thousand Hungarians gathered on Lajos Kossuth Square, protesting against Márton Gyöngyösi, the leader of Jobbik, the third biggest party in the Hungarian parliament. Gyöngyösi had declared the need to compile a list of Jews who posed potential security threats to the country. Seeing Budapest residents, their coats emblazoned with handsewn yellow stars in protest, was a harrowing experience. According to the city's Holocaust Memorial Centre, between five and six hundred thousand Hungarian Jews perished in the concentration camps. Jobbik owes its rise in the polls to anti-Semitism and its open hatred of Roma, some seven hundred thousand of whom live in Hungary—and who don't have any place else to go. Because Roma,

well, everyone hates Roma: the Serbs, the Croats, the Czechs, the
Slovaks, the Romanians, the Bulgarians, everyone . . .

In early December 2012, I rode the single daily train between Budapest and Zagreb. There used to be an Osijek-Budapest line, but now
that's gone too. People say trains are too expensive.

It was this irreparable feeling of absence that settled in me in
Gyékényes, on the border between Hungary and Croatia. It was
as if Gyékényes was the edge of the world, and that nothing came
after. The carriages emptied (is really no one traveling to Croatia?),
and the Croatian border guard stamped my Dutch passport, his
movements lumbering, the stamp moist and cold. And then darkness enveloped Gyékényes. Dim station lights shone in Koprivnica,
Križevci, Vrbovac, and Dugo Selo. Everything else was lost in the
murky black. Watching the pale light seeping from the tiny station
office in Vrbovac, that's what I thought about, the collocation *murky
black*.

At some point the train stopped. A middle-aged woman appeared
from a neighboring compartment.

"Where are we?" she asked, as if in an amateur theater production.

There being no answer from anywhere, she dared give it another
go.

"Where are we now?"

Again there was no reply, and the woman, chastened somehow,
withdrew into her compartment.

I took a taxi from the railway station, and heading toward Novi
Zagreb noticed a billboard for *Intimissimi* lingerie. In the murky

black above Zagreb, giant supermodels floated in panties and bras, laid out on their sides, heads resting on a hand, staring out into the endless murk ahead . . .

7.

Zagreb is a city that often comes a halt, and then just stays there. In Croatia there is a tunnel that leads nowhere, just stops dead, right there in a hillside. One of Zagreb's most well-known streets, Savska, stops being a proper street before it even gets going; Ilica, one of Zagreb's main thoroughfares, is also barely urban. Perhaps this explains Zagreb's terminal moroseness, the inspiration for countless chansons poeticizing its absence of content, its tired urban imagery: street lights, old lanterns, the banks of the Sava (which the city stubbornly ignores), parks, pigeons, and clay-tiled roofs. In this endless poeticization of return (*I'm coming back, oh Zagreb, to you, you on the banks of the Sava* . . .), the poetic voice is always out there on the road somewhere, his return to Zagreb a sounding of the alarm. Zagreb is a deaf and indifferent urban stain, its pulse barely discernable as the poet whinnies his return.

I remember my first longer absence from Zagreb. There was no such thing as the Internet, international phone calls were expensive, letters the sole means of communication. Return was cause for real celebration. My three best friends awaited me at the airport, and we headed straight over to my mom's, my mom having prepared a special lunch. My friends nattered away merrily, attempting enchantment with stories of everything that had happened while I'd been away. At one moment I burst into tears. My friends excused themselves, oh, she must be really tired, let's go, we'll leave you to rest up, let's catch up tomorrow . . . I don't really remember what was said anymore, it wasn't important. But I didn't burst out crying because I was tired, I burst out crying at the regime of the Zagreb everyday, leaking from my friends' mouths like unsightly mucus. I burst out crying because of the absence of content, because of their absence of interest in anything beyond their own lives. My friends never asked what I'd been up to in the ten months I'd been away. Zagreb fell on my cheek like a dollop of indifferent spit.

The Yugoslav *Gastarbeiter* of the seventies know the story well, as do the flood of Yugoslav refugees of the nineties; every returnee learns it some day. Either you are here with us, or you don't exist. It is a cast-iron rule. And it is why every time I go back to Zagreb, slowly, like a reconvalescent, I practice the rituals of return. In Zagreb I have my pedicurist, a heroine whose handiwork supports an unemployed husband and three school-age sons. As she struggles to keep her head above water, my periodic appearance works like an oxygen mask—I see it in her eyes and smile. At the nearby market I buy eggs from the same statuesque woman, who, adorned by chicken feathers, keeps the day's takings in a tin can, the lid of which bears stickers of the Virgin Mary and Severina,[1] the two women *my* egg seller worships. I visit my dentist, who isn't actually my dentist anymore, he's retired, but I like to sit down in his chair, and for us to talk, about his grandchildren, about mutual acquaintances, some of whom already lie buried. I go to my hairdresser, even though she does a wonky job; I go to my seamstress, even though she's sloppy and charges the earth. All offer me a vague warmth. They are my measure of Zagreb, as much as I can handle; nothing too exciting, nothing that hurts.

---

1   Severina Vučković, the most popular Croatian pop singer, known also as Seve Nacionale, or simply Seve.

The rest is just sadness, a sadness that comes from helplessness, from watching a little crappy homemade porn, from a cheap betrayal, from the realization that we've been had, that the streets are full of shell-game cons, that we've played having consented to losing in advance, and that we would've been conned even if we hadn't played; it's the suffocating sadness that comes from a momentary glimmer of hope that all is not lost, that, for fuck's sake, all can't be lost, and the realization that this record has been stuck for years, that all really is lost; it's the sadness that comes from cheap revenge, from the realization that someone's spat in our soup, that they've been at it for years, and don't even themselves know why; the sadness that overwhelms us on sighting curtains with ingrained filth, from the stench of piss in our nostrils, feline and human; a sadness whose sheer weight knocks us to the ground, a sadness born of a realization of the banality of human evil, an evil that sucks the oxygen from our lungs . . .

8.

Merry Christmas to our veterans and heroes in prison!—a banner snakes through Zagreb's main square. A dozen or so men, war veterans presumably, support the banner. War veterans, volunteers, they're a new breed, ghosted in from invisible wings to occupy center stage in Croatian life, a breed of man who voluntarily took up arms to fight a "defensive" war. When the war was over, they got themselves organized, started up all kinds of associations seeking recompense— pensions, apartments, jobs—for their voluntary entanglements. The state has paid them the deepest financial and moral respect. For many veterans, the four-year war has become an identity, a biography, a career, a raison d'être. A handful of associations (and the odd individual) spent years pestering the relevant military organs to make the veteran register public, and in December 2012—twenty years after the fact—it finally was. It turned out that the figure of half a million, which had long provoked disbelief, was indeed correct. It also turned out that almost a third of those on the register had faked their service. In recent years the number of veterans on invalid's pensions has increased by around forty percent. An invalid's pension is more than a regular veteran's. And a veteran's pension is more than a non-veteran's pension. All told, the average veteran's pension is twice that of a university professor.

This is another fairytale of success, Croatian-style. Get yourself in among the vets, and you've won a place at the very heart of the Croatian state, your mitts on the sword and cross. The slogan—*Merry Christmas to our veterans and heroes in prison!*—is season's greetings to all those still in detention in the Hague, those waiting in pre-trial detention in Croatia, maybe even to fraudsters like former Croatian prime minister Ivo Sanader, who, accused of corruption, is out on bail. Those accused of heroic corruption, they were defending the homeland too.

Even the façade of Zagreb's new Museum of Modern Art bears the graffito *Ante Gotovina—hero*. At Christmas 2012, master carver Josip Mateša fashioned a life-size nativity scene. Next to a wooden statue of the Virgin Mary stood a wooden statue of Ante Gotovina in his general's uniform, Croatian flag in hand. As the wooden Jesus slept peacefully in his wooden crib, Mateša told the papers that he'd chosen Ante Gotovina as a "symbol of righteous struggle." He didn't, of course, go into the specifics of who or what this "righteous struggle" was waged against. A newspaper photo, with a general's cap placed over the crib where wooden baby Jesus lay, suggests that Ante Gotovina might well be Jesus's symbolic father. Master carver Mateša obviously had something similar in mind. Given the Croatian Catholic leadership's adoration of Ante Gotovina, and Ante Gotovina's reciprocal adoration of the clergy, the Church silently acquiesced to this original artistic intervention.

Croatian performance artist Marijan Crtalić probably won't make it into the Museum of Modern Art. He is, in any case, seeking exit, not entry. In one of his pieces, "The Possibility of Exit," he tries to bang his head through a wall. Literally. In another piece, "The World Should Know that a Croat Loves His People," he attempts singing the national anthem with his hands bound, and tape across his mouth. Crtalić's self-harm is artistic protest against state violence against the individual.

9.

Is it only the Croatian Catholic Church that is shameless, or is every church, ipso facto, such? The Croatian church is fed at a trough filled by the Croatian taxpayer, and despite being the wealthiest institution in the country (owing to its vast real estate holdings), it sucks the taxpayer's teet dry. In Croatia, eighty-seven percent of citizens identify as Catholics. In other words, the Croatian everyman decides how much money should be allocated to the Church, and how much to his children's education. With the Croatian congregation having cast its public doors wide open, the Church wasted no time marching straight on into the education system, the very heart of things. Although grade school religious instruction is supposedly voluntary, it's Clayton's choice—I mean, when have young children ever been able to decide this sort of thing for themselves? And the Church marched on: into secondary schools, universities and other educational institutions, into hospitals, courtrooms, the media, political structures—its influence insidious. In December 2012, the Church used every propaganda means at its disposal to attack a draft bill introducing human development and sex education into the school curriculum, with sectarian groups, the media, newsagents, and even a supermarket chain owned by a Croatian oligarch all offering assistance. The Church, which maintains a relentless campaign against homosexuality, the use of contraception, pre-marital sex, and the like, claims that sex education goes against its teachings. Citing the Pope, the Church sounded its bugle to the Croatian flock that they reject totalitarian attitudes and thinking. Introducing human development classes in schools is apparently a *totalitarian act*, sex education both *anti-Croatian* and *anti-Catholic*. That is the Church's official position.

10.

I recently watched Nenad Puhovski's documentary *Pavilion 22*, ten years after it was made. The film was only ever shown on the festival circuit, never on television. While judges at the Hague tribunal watched it as evidence, the wider Croatian public isn't aware of its existence. Yet this general public isn't completely oblivious to the "terrifying things" that took place at the Zagreb exhibition center in 1991. Several years after the fact, one of those directly involved, Miro Bajramović, gave an interview to the *Feral Tribune* weekly, in which he claimed that he himself had killed some seventy-six people, the majority Serbs. The case was hushed up, Bajramović dismissed as mentally unsound. Ten years later, however, police arrested six men, four of whom were released after questioning, while Bajramović and another man were eventually sentenced to relatively brief prison terms, most of which they served in pre-trial detention. All of the film's protagonists, except the former minister of police and one Tomislav Merčep, the chief suspect, testified to the existence of notorious paramilitary units. Croatian jails emptied their cells as the war began. Apparently that's the thing to do in wartime. Serving prisoners become "dogs of war." Some formed paramilitary groups, one of which was led by Merčep. The documentary's subjects maintain that Merčep's "pack" tortured, raped, and brutalized (mostly) Croatian Serbs, before transporting them to Pakračka Poljana, where they were murdered. A hall at the Zagreb exhibition center functioned as a private detention camp, where the dogs of war engaged in "operational processing." It seems many people knew what was going on, about the crimes being committed, but no one lifted a finger to intervene. The minister of police at the time defended Merčep's "dogs," claiming that they had performed an "enormous service." He didn't go into the precise nature of what this "enormous service" entailed. It took twenty years and constant pressure from Amnesty International for the Croatian judiciary to finally indict Merčep, who was arrested in 2010. The indictment accused him of commanding a paramilitary unit responsible for the 1991 murder of forty-three civilians and the disappearance of a further three persons. It stated that he knew about the extrajudicial arrests, the terror, abuse, torture, and execution of civilians, and that he did nothing to prevent it. His trial continues.

11.

An old friend had stubbornly refused to take me with him, and then one day he finally relented.

"There's nothing to see, unless you want to look at people neck-deep in the shit, and in that case, be my guest!" he said. Today, in a hall of the Zagreb exhibition center, welfare packets are distributed to "special cases." The bureaucracy, the media, and even those stigmatized as such, use the expression, one that adroitly quarantines a much wider despair. Because in reality, most of the population is barely getting by; it's the rich who are "special cases." Like many Croatians, my friend has slipped from the ranks of the former middle class down into those of the special cases. Many "cases" have advanced qualifications, yet as losers in the transition, are too young for retirement and too old for retraining. My friend spent his working life in two big companies—the first, a state-owned enterprise in the time when Yugoslavia was still whole, the second, a private Croatian-owned firm in the post-independence period. The director of the latter was a typical transition hustler. He got the firm cheap via political connections. In time he turned the employees into his personal slaves, and ceased making statutory contributions to their health insurance and retirement schemes. Then he started paying a quarter of his employees' wages out in vouchers, vouchers only valid in a handful of supermarkets. Then he dropped hourly rates to minimum wage, and after that, he started paying half that minimum wage out in vouchers. And now the vouchers could only be redeemed at the firm itself. The company sold construction material, which in practice meant that employees could exchange their vouchers for toilet seats and bathroom tiles. The director wasn't entirely without a social conscience, so he started stocking his shelves with pasta, *Eurokrem*, and tinned goods past their expiration dates. Employees could get hold of foodstuffs, albeit at twice the price of other stores. Of course at other stores, their vouchers were no good.

The owner of the firm abused his employees in every which way, all in the hope that they'd quit of their own volition, because otherwise, at least according to the statute book, he'd have to pay a severance. He didn't let anyone go. And then, when the recession had bitten hard, he started laying people off without paying them redundancy money, knowing full well that the Croatian judiciary is paleolithic, and that even if someone did sue, it would take years to get a verdict against him. No one sued. Apart from the cleaner; she accused him of raping her in the toilet. To general amazement, the court believed her. But even this seemed to work in the owner's favor. Sentences for rape are much lighter than those for embezzlement, corruption, and racketeering. In the sea of criminality, rape is considered shenanigans for grown-up little boys. My friend is on the unemployment agency's books, and the welfare line. The owner of the firm, he's a free man. He hasn't gotten around to serving his time.

I watched this friend of mine race to fill his box with household essentials, a big bag of cornflakes, two or three kilos of flour, sugar, and oil, a kilo of bacon, a marble cake, half a kilo of cheese . . . in sum, a Christmas present from Ebenezer Scrooge. I watched him hurry out with his cardboard box, stash it the trunk, and turn the ignition. Any stoppage, any delay would mean confronting his own position, and he doesn't want that. Christ, anything but that. Silent as shadows, he and his people turn up here once a month to collect their care packages. If they don't show on the day of the month assigned to them, they permanently lose the right to further assistance.

"Everything looks normal, much more civilized than one would think," I say, trying to break the silence.

"That's the problem, everything *looks* normal," he replied.

Twenty years ago, the dogs of war "worked over" their Serb compatriots in one of the exhibition center halls. Today, twenty years after the establishment of the sovereign Republic of Croatia, many Croatian citizens—stripped to their undies by their ethnic brothers, their fellow Croats—come here to gather crumbs from under the table.

12.

"Everyone knows Dora's aunty!"

"Who is she?"

"She's on TV!"

"Ah . . ."

"You're a writer . . ."

"I think I am."

"Then why aren't you in our school books?"

"Would you like me to be?"

"I would!"

"I'm sorry, sweetheart . . ."

"Even our teacher hasn't heard of you!"

"Well, if your teacher had read anything, she would have!"

"Our teacher reads heaps, but you're not in the shops, or in the library, or on TV . . . If you were, our teacher would know!"

On December 27, 2012, a regular episode of the show *TV kalendar* aired on Croatian state television. There was a segment in which an Ustasha war criminal by the name of Jure Francetić was hailed as a "legendary fighter." In the same segment the Partisans were characterized as a criminal band, running amok in the hills, slaughtering Croats. The only protest against this historical revisionism came from a small NGO called the Citizens' Initiative. It's hard for a handful of people to kick against the system. Especially when the system consists of publishers, editors, newspapers, television, radio, teachers, university lecturers, historians, and journalists—all of them engaged in peddling this sort of thing. Why? Because they can. Because they think they're right. Because they want to please someone who thinks he's right. But can we conceive of a primetime show on German television declaring the Holocaust a historical fabrication, six million murdered Jews an exaggeration, and Adolf Eichmann the greatest German humanitarian of all time?

In 2012, a group of young Croatian filmmakers shot a short documentary simply entitled *Who Are They?* The film captures responses to the titular question by ordinary Zagreb residents living near an improvised shelter for refugees. Asked to describe the refugees in their neighborhood, one replied that were *dark*; another suggested *well-baked*; a third *pretty dark-skinned*; a fourth that *they're not folk like us*; a fifth that *there are more and more of them*; a sixth that *every piece of shit comes to us*; while a seventh, a young man with an easy smile, remarked that *they closed Jasenovac, so I don't know what we're supposed to do with them!*[2]

A people who in the twenty years of their state sovereignty has desecrated or destroyed three thousand monuments to the victims of fascism, burned almost three million books[3] and "reduced" the Serbian ethnic minority by half, is now writing its history, a history of pure, untainted souls, of hardworking and honest folk who believe in one God. The rest is just collateral damage. People are as mindless as flies; stuck in the collective glue, they think they got there of their own free will. The brutalized girl, she's collateral damage too, the corpse of a mindless fly in a sticky-sweet national flytrap . . .

---

2   "The Jasenovac concentration camp was a site of imprisonment, forced labor, and liquidation, primarily of the Serbian Orthodox population, which, in order to create an ethically clean territory, had to be completely eradicated from the Independent State of Croatia, as did Jews and Roma, who were also discriminated against under racial laws. A significant number of Croats—communists and anti-fascists, members of the National Liberation Army of Croatia, their families, and other opponents of the Ustasha regime—also perished in the camp." (www.jusp-jasenovac.hr)

3   See Ante Lešaja's *Bibliocide: the Destruction of Books in Croatia in the 1990s.*

The same day Croatian hero Ante Gotovina touched down, in Podstrana a young girl was brutally raped. She and her friends had been celebrating Gotovina's release. The rape of a girl, the blood of a virgin, is a little pagan offering to merciless gods. Residents of Pakoštane, Ante Gotovina's birthplace, turned out to celebrate divine justice, slaughtering a fattened calf. Rape suspect Roko Šimac was released from investigative detention after a month and a half. Blood analysis showed that the group of young partygoers had not been under the influence of drugs. They were just drunk. The girl whose internal organs were ripped apart was released from the hospital for outpatient care. They say she still doesn't remember anything.

Let's go back to the beginning of the story: No one cares about temporal coordinates any more, not when something happened, not what happened. The clock was violently wound back twenty years ago. Franjo Tuđman was the first to mess with its hands, successfully erasing fifty years of Yugoslav social life and state sovereignty, grafting his Croatia onto the Ustasha puppet state of the Second World War. Tuđman managed to salvage and restore many icons of the era: the coat of arms, the flag, the currency, turns of phrase, and much else besides. Hence the temporal disorder that suits some so well. Because temporal confusion allows criminals to not answer for their crimes, nor murders for their murderers, thieves for their thefts, rapists for their rapes. Only in temporal confusion can victims claim they don't remember anything.

13.

My niece and I are sitting in the back seat. Her dad is driving. We're coming home from a children's birthday party. We pass a lingerie advertisement. A beauty in a bra and panties lies stretched out on her side, her head supported by her hand, her indifferent eyes staring out into the murk of the horizon . . .

"Look, Aunty, a Croatian fairy . . ." my niece murmurs, bleary-eyed at the billboard that has just sprung up in front of her.

"Yes, sweetheart, the fairy of all Croats . . ." I say. She's already asleep. She's sunken into a sweet dream, as if into the salty sea.

THE MUSEUM
OF TOMORROW

1.

A taxi driver was waiting for me at London Heathrow, holding a piece of paper with my name on it. He introduced himself and kissed my hand. Never in my life has a taxi driver kissed my hand. Carlos, he said his name was Carlos. He was a small man, with a round face and hazel eyes like marbles. As we drove my eyes fell on his chubby little hands. He's just a teddy bear, a living toy, I thought. His voice silky and soft, restrained, almost feminine.

Carlos was Romanian, from a small provincial town, and unsurprisingly his name wasn't actually Carlos, it was Octavius. "Octavius" had had the guys from the taxi co-op in stitches, so they called him Carlos. He lives in London, shares a tiny flat with another couple of Romanians, five hundred pounds a month, all he can afford. He's divorced; in Romania he's got an ex-wife and a teenage daughter. Over here he met a Romanian woman with a similar story, with an ex-husband and a teenage son. He wants to start a new life with her, with Nausica. In London? London's not bad, but no, not in London.

So where then? In Australia, somewhere on the east coast, near the ocean . . . Communism was good, because with the chronic lack of other amusements, people read a lot. As a kid he adored Jules Verne. All of us, us "Easterners," we adored Jules Verne. In one of Verne's books he'd stumbled across a description of Australia, a description now imprinted in his brain like a barcode. It's true that right now it all seems like a distant dream; there's a heap of bureaucratic hurdles to overcome, among other things, he wants to take his daughter with him, and she, the love of his life, her son. But he's sure that one day he and Nausica will end up out there in Australia, somewhere near Great Barrier Reef, in the Coral Sea . . .

"In communism we dreamed a lot, and that was the best part about it," he said, as if drawing silk from between his lips.

Carlos dropped me off at the hotel, carried my luggage right to the reception desk, and handed me his business card with the number of his taxi firm.

"If you need a taxi on the way back, call this number. And don't forget, it's Carlos, ask for Carlos . . ." he said, imparting a little dry kiss on my clumsy hand.

2.

A sixty-something woman, her bearing unusually upright, long straight gray hair, a smattering of coquettish afro plaits, her face lined and tanned as if she spends most of the day outside. Blue, expressionless eyes, a gaze that never meets her interlocutor, a yoga bunny, for sure . . . Her voice sounds calmly from her lips, she's happy with her life, her lot; true, things went downhill a bit when her brother died, she adopted his son, but then he died too, now she doesn't have anyone, her mom's dead, but at least she made it to the ripe old age of eighty-eight. Yes, it's true, people around her are disappearing, yesterday they were here, today they're no more. She spits the last phrase out resolutely, flicks her long gray locks and abandons the subject. She gesticulates wildly, as if wanting to bat her interlocutor's stare from her face. She flaps her arms like wings, shooing away prying eyes. Of course she's working, she's got heaps to work on, projects and stuff, yeah, she was just there, there too, but now she's off somewhere else, and after that . . .

3.

They put their bare legs up on the chair, caress the smooth skin of their calves, massage their toes, and then grab their phones, stroking and caressing them as they just did their calves. They laugh, flash healthy, toothy smiles, throw their hair back, twirling curls in their fingers. They take chomping bites, like on TV—you know the show, the one with an anorexic actress feigning a wolf's appetite. They murmur their mmmmmms, sigh, their mouths full, gourmand pleasure in overdrive. They've got tinny, almost metallic whines. Cartoongirls. Tiny fingers, slender as birds' claws, they tap away, enamored with the screens on their phones. From time to time they shoot out a brisk glance, not looking at anyone or anything, just like hens.

4.

There's a guy on the plane, in the seat in front of mine, radiant with a wretch's delight. Having bought a ticket, the seat's all his for a whole two hours. He makes himself right at home, and then for some reason starts beating the back of his head against the head rest, once, twice, thrice. He must be checking if he's still alive, whether the head rest is really his, or maybe he just wants the back of his head to make the acquaintance of the kind of head rests you get in planes. Christ, who would know what this creature wants. Maybe he doesn't want anything, maybe his body is making the seat's acquaintance of its own accord. He just wriggles away, exploring the space around him. Here we go—he finds the button on the side and reclines his seat with a jerk. At that very moment I've just opened my tray and put my book and plastic cup of coffee down. The steaming coffee ends up in my lap. The second the plane touches down he'll be first up, opening the overhead locker, getting his stuff out, Duty Free crap, this much I know. And I automatically hunch my shoulders, because his stuff is already falling on my head . . . Somewhere from a seat behind me there's a woman's laugh, a strange sentence nibbling my ear: *It must be that gall stone I had removed that's making me laugh.*

5.

I put my odds and ends down on the counter. The checkout girl punches in the prices, pausing at the kohlrabi. She frowns, waving it at a colleague:

"You know what this is?"

"No idea."

She looks inquiringly at me, but I just shrug, I'm not telling her what it's called. The line behind me sucks up her confusion. In the end a woman in line loses patience and yells out . . .

"Kohlrabi! It's kohlrabi, for Christ's sake!"

The checkout girl finds the name and code number and swiftly enters the price.

At home I take the kohlrabi and drown it in warm water together with my freezing hands. I think how the same scene with the kohlrabi has already played out three times, and that each time it was a different checkout girl. Then I take a knife and carefully peel the kohlrabi. Kohlrabi, "German beet," *kohlrübe, knolkhol, nookal, gedde kosu, navilu kosu, moonji, munji haakh . . .*

Then I wonder whether checkout girls should know the names of everything they sell. And I wonder how is it that they're not even curious. But I let it go, I realize I'm asking too much. Most checkout girls are just kids, I mean, they look like kids. A lot of them wear hijabs. Why do I think they should care about some old beet they don't even eat? Their fates are already long settled, pre-coded, a checkout girl is herself a commodity, already imprinted with a barcode, *strichcode, code a barres, codice a barre, čarovy kod* . . . Yes, soon she'll find a little man, bear his children, and one day those kids will have the run of the supermarket. Alongside the supermarket the benevolent city fathers will build a children's playground, and benches, so grandmas and grandpas can sit down while they watch the kids play, while Mama's at work at the supermarket, while Mama's doing the shopping. There'll be temples a short stroll away, one, two, three, for every faith a temple. Life is arranged in such a way that it can't be better—here, we've everything we need. Old men in long white robes sit on the benches, drawing bread from plastic bags. With languid, beatific waves they toss out little pieces, feeding the visible pigeons and invisible rats. Maybe they're sitting there thinking that every being on earth deserves to eat its fill; that every being on earth should know its species and breed, its name and its price . . .

6.

A chance glance at the chintzy gold anklet and the butt rammed into stretchy jeans triggered an attack of misanthropy that left me breathless. The foot was in a see-through nylon stocking in a high-heeled sandal, the cheap nylon shading the anklet's golden shine, ragged heel, and red nail polish. Getting up, the butt and gold anklet strode off toward the bathroom.

7.

"You know, not everyone who speaks Bulgarian is Bulgarian," Meli offers cautiously. She's actually trying to tell me that she's a Bulgarian Turk. For some reason Meli thinks this is important. She came to Amsterdam to work as a cleaner, she barely finished grade school, which is partly explained by the fact that she's got seventeen siblings. It seems her parents were born to procreate, and the second they were done, began decomposing like salmon after mating. Her father died, and like some matriarchal goddess, her mother lies wasting away in a Turkish village in northeastern Bulgaria, the clan's young tending to her. Meli cleans Dutch houses and apartments. She lives in a rented Amsterdam apartment with three sisters and a brother. They all earn their keep cleaning and thus support the extended family. Meli's never traveled anywhere, doesn't know any place besides Amsterdam and her native village. She's never been to Sofia. It's not quite that she never thinks of herself though, she's bought herself a house in the village, next to those of her older sisters. She's slowly furnishing it. She's twenty-two years old, but she's not thinking of getting married, she's too old. She chuckles and admits that she can't remember the names of all her brothers and sisters.

8.

Wioleta Sroka, she says, accosting me at the airport. It's me, your assistant. There are heaps of other volunteers, but I wanted to be assigned to you, you and no one else. We're the ABBA generation, you and me, aren't we?

Mrs. Sroka is a heavyset middle-aged woman with long, disheveled hair dyed flaming red. The cut, the bangs, the limp locks falling halfway down her back, it's a look she hasn't changed since the seventies. She must have been pretty when she was young. She's still got that primary accumulation of self-confidence of those who where physically attractive in their youth. She talks a lot, her voice croaky. She's also got that smoker's fan of ancient fine lines above her lips, yet for whatever reason is quick to tell me that she's never smoked a cigarette in her life.

She doesn't leave my side, barges into my hotel room uninvited, scopes the place out—the hotel is new, it's got five stars, that's irrelevant, you know how sloppy they build these days . . . She obviously has no intention of going anywhere, heads out onto the balcony, checks out the view, insists on waiting while I get ready. To go where? To the formal opening of the congress. No, I say, I'm exhausted from the trip, I'd rather stay in. Shall I wait for you in the lobby? No, thanks, there's no need, I say. It's as if she's going to burst into tears. Fine, I'll come and get you tomorrow morning, she says, almost offended.

She doesn't leave me alone for a second. When I meet other conference guests she takes a bunch of business cards from her bag, handing them out indiscriminately. *That's me*, she says, running her finger under the name on the card. She hands me a bunch too. She's got green ones and yellow ones, which would I prefer? She stands guard for me outside the restroom, like she's scared I'll give her the slip. She looks like a former ABBA groupie, a gone-to-seed Agnetha clone.

She's constantly inserting herself in the frame, chin-wagging with the TV crew, *that's me*, she parrots, palming off her business cards and running her finger under her name. *That's me!* As the camera starts to roll she fixes my scarf. There, she says, satisfied.

Apparently it's time I ate. I try to abscond with an acquaintance for lunch. No luck, she and I go to lunch together. She's a widow, her second husband died recently. She doesn't go on annual vacation, what's the point of annual vacations when you're on your own? Better to volunteer for stuff like this, it's way more interesting, and besides, she's a poet herself, she publishes in literary magazines. She pulls out a thin volume of poetry, placing it in front of me. *That's me*, she says, pointing at the name on the cover. Yes, she's got two sons from her first marriage, they're big boys, she's already a grandmother, but she doesn't see her boys much, they rarely call. She's retired, but you can't live on three hundred euro a month. She and her mother combine their two pensions and somehow survive.

Her second husband was an angel, a real angel, they met at clay pigeon shooting . . . What? Clay pigeon shooting, people get together and shoot clay pigeons. Here you go, that's him, she says, taking a picture from her wallet. A good-natured chump in a hunting jacket and hat looks up at me from the picture. There's a feather in the hat, a feathery souvenir fallen from a mighty angel's wing. They were married for five years and he went within six months, pancreatic cancer . . . She's been on her own since then, lives with her ninety-two-year-old mother. Mom's doing okay, everyone in the family lives to a ripe old age, it's in our genetic code, she says. She's decided to just get on and be happy with her life, her lot, to stay active. She insists we have a photo together, just me and her, then her, then me and the students, then her, then me and some folks who came to the reading, then her, me, and the acquaintance I caught up with at the congress . . .

I recently came across a photo on the Internet. Wioleta Sroka and me, a couple of gone-to-seed ABBA groupies, Frida and Agnetha.

We're standing there on some steps leading to God only knows
where . . .

9.

Caught in motion, the fragments assembled here are randomly stored
images: a gesture, body, phrase, way of behaving, tone of voice, a
snippet of conversation, a haphazard and disconnected internal slide
show. Only in retrospect do I see the common associative thread:
Not one of these images is happy—though it's true that none is
particularly unhappy.

We dreamed a lot in communism, and that was the best part about it,
said Carlos, my slip of a taxi driver. This best part will never find
a place in any museum of communism for the simple reason that
it's intangible: It crouches hiding in literature, in film, in painting,
in the architecture of an epoch that believed it was creating a new
world. In turn this new world gave birth to a new art, a good part
of which spent its life in the underground, because the world that
created it quickly lost any connection to the real existing one. The
art in question had an oneiric power. The other truth is that many
of its consumers were dreamers too.

In Rio de Janeiro, Santiago Calatrava is building a museum that
promises to be one of the most beautiful buildings in the world:
the *Museu do Amanhã*, the Museum of Tomorrow. The museum's
content will apparently be devoted to the "eco-sustainable development of the planet." Couched in this kind of bureaucratese, the content doesn't seem particularly alluring, perhaps because the oneiric
architectural beauty of the future museum is—in and of itself—the
content. The very name of the museum trips a light in the future
visitor's head, bringing to mind many things: the awareness that

man inhabits a planet surrounded by other planets; the awareness that there is a future for which we are responsible, for which we refuse any responsibility, the future being something that presently worries us least; the awareness that one day future inhabitants of the earth will judge us, that this judgment will be in accord with what we have bequeathed to them, the kind of world we have passed down as an inheritance, the art, music, living spaces, literature, the kind of people, cities, parks, values . . . Yet it's entirely possible that things are much simpler than this. Perhaps only a country that believes it has a tomorrow (even if this tomorrow is named the 2016 Olympic Games) dares build museums.

"Europe no longer loves life," Peter Sloterdijk said somewhere. "The radiance of historical fulfilment is gone, in its place only exhaustion, the entropic qualities of an aging culture," a reign of "spiritual nakedness." Is our epoch really "a time of empty angels"?[1] What messages does the European today send out to the Europe of tomorrow?

If one were to ask me, as a writer I would, perhaps predictably, immediately think about human beings, of a record of everyday human lives, something akin to a perfect (and perfectly monstrous!) archive for future readers, its files taking account of the smallest details of the lives of regular, anonymous people, like the archive of

---

1 "The time of empty angels is a syndrome in which everyone wants to be a messenger, yet no one makes the least effort to receive the messages of others; everyone wants to cut through the clatter and be heard, be in the control room, get something into print, but unfortunately they've got nothing to say. This syndrome, with its unheard messages, results in media nihilism. Working in tandem, the means of transmitting these forgotten messages only increases." Interview with Peter Sloterdijk, *Zarez*, 19 (1999), 12-13; *Magazine litteraire*, September 1999.)

Danilo Kiš's *The Encyclopedia of the Dead*, inspired by a newspaper report on the Mormon archives.

Yet when I try to put myself in Carlos's position, that of a consumer of dreams, I immediately change tack, and choose the Museo Nazionale del Cinema in Turin as my launch pad for broadcasting messages to the future. It's cosy, sensual, and wired with oneiric energy.

Yes, the National Museum of Cinema in Turin. Flopping down into a recliner in which you lie more than sit, we place headphones over our ears, direct our eyes high toward the cupola of the Mole Antonelliana—one of Turin's strangest structures—and watch the inaudible slide of the panoramic glass lift, full of visitors, descending from or ascending to the lookout point at the cupola's peak. Having ourselves ridden in that same glass cage, we observe others on their gentle vertical slide, up and down. We are no longer participants, but observers.

Lying down, headphones over our ears, we immerse ourselves in a huge canvas as clips from Europe's neglected film history are beamed before us. We catapult ourselves into the world of images, and swaddled in the imagined future like a mouse in cheese, we observe our recent past. God, look at them all: Luis Buñuel, Federico Fellini, Ingmar Bergman, Lina Wertmüller, Liliana Cavani, Jean-Luc Godard, Miloš Forman, Sergei Eisenstein, Krzysztof Kieślowski, Bernardo Bertolucci, Michelangelo Antonioni, Jiří Menzel, Jeanne Moreau, Simone Signoret, Anna Magnani, Giulietta Masina, and scores of others—where did they all disappear to? And I think, seen from some future perspective, isn't it the case that cinema—and not literature, music, or visual art—is the most powerful and enthralling legacy of our epoch?

And so we sit and watch the film assembled for museum visitors by Gianni Amelio, a montage of dance scenes from European and American films. With the force of a laser, these dancing images smash loose the deposits of misanthropy that in the accumulated years have clogged my veins. It now seems that I know the content of the message that, if called upon, I would send out into the future, to a museum of tomorrow. My message would consist of images of couples dancing—not of "dancing with the stars"—but the dancing of ordinary people projected into the sky like stars.[2] The message would be accompanied by a single caption, Amanda Wingfield's heartbreaking line from Irving Raper's 1950 film adaptation of Tennessee Williams's *The Glass Menagerie*: "I've always said that dancing is the most civilized form of social intercourse."

---

2   Ettore Scola's silent film *Le Bal* (1983) features couples as they dance their way through almost the entire twentieth century, proof enough, if one is so inclined, that history (in this case, recent European history) can be easily portrayed from the interior of a dance hall, by gesture, music, and movement.

MANIFESTO

1. A VIDEO CLIP

A Zagreb acquaintance recently sent me a YouTube clip that's been
making the rounds. It's actually a newsreel chronicling Zagreb's
economic triumphs between 1967 and 1969, and was originally used
as propaganda in city councilors' re-election campaigns. Well into
the 70s, newsreels would play in movie theaters before the feature,
just like the ads and trailers we get today.

The voiceover and images tell a phenomenal success story. In the
given two-year period, the city built new factories, schools, hospital wards, kindergartens, roads, new residential settlements—the
graphics, numbers, and statistics are all there to prove it. My Zagreb
acquaintance tells me that today, forty years later, the clip has been
an online sensation in Croatia. Why? What could be so gripping
about an old Yugoslav (socialist) puff piece? Its truthfulness. What?!
Yes—it's the truthfulness of it that gets people. All those factories
really were built, and what's more, some of them became Yugoslavia's

biggest exporters; the schools, residential blocks and neighborhoods, they were built too. In 1972, my parents bought a fourteenth-floor apartment in one such "skyscraper." Watching the clip, I recognized both my old neighborhood and my future skyscraper. I still remember the joy the amazing fourteenth-floor view out over empty fields provoked in me. From time to time, new clusters of tower blocks rose from the fields, stretching up toward the horizon. All this happened within the space of some fifteen (communist) years.

The Internet is like the ocean—every day it washes new debris upon the shore. The clip in question is just one such piece of detritus. Viewed by anyone able to claim it as part of his or her own mental baggage, it's bound to prompt a reaction. My Zagreb acquaintance complains that her husband just sits there on YouTube all day, watching the clip over and over, bawling his eyes out. "He's completely lost his marbles! How can someone cry over a bunch of sepia shots of factory halls?!" she protests. Her husband used to work at the factory. In the "transition" period it went belly-up, and he was forced to take early retirement.

People cry for all kinds of reasons, most often when confronted by their own defeat. "Twenty years they've been feeding us crap on TV, in the papers. The media used to be much better quality," a first person says. "Life itself, the one we had in Yugoslavia, used to be better quality," a second chimes in. "Why did we march off to war then?" a third asks. "What war? You, old fella, are lost in time. That was twenty years ago," a fourth responds. "This ongoing idioticization of the people is becoming unbearable. Politicians have fried our brains, and soon they're gonna toss us in the trash," a fifth adds. "We're already in the trash," a sixth comes back at him.

"It's what we deserve for being such fools!" a seventh concludes. "It's comforting to know that we're not the only idiots. Look at the Italians. All the shit they've been through, how can anyone still vote for Berlusconi?!" an eighth observes. "Put up and shut up, that's all that's left for us," a ninth summarizes. "Right on, voting is a complete crock anyhow! What's the point, we're already dead," a tenth fires.

"You're drawing the wrong conclusions. It's got nothing to do with the fact that we've been betrayed by both systems, by communism and capitalism. Personally, I can start bawling for no reason at all, it's enough for me to watch National Geographic and the tear ducts burst. We're all depressed, believe me," another acquaintance tells me. He's forty-five years old, single, pays his bills on time, is gainfully employed.

Once two zones separated by a pretty decent wall, in the space of twenty years Europe has become a chaotic mega-market. There are now no walls, and no coordinates either; no one knows where the West is, and where the East. The West is settling in the East, the East surging into the West, the North heading South, and the South, well, it's mulling its options. Young Spaniards are abandoning their homeland en masse; young Greeks seeking out relatives long dispersed to far corners of the earth; trying to extract themselves from the ever-widening quicksand, young Croats recently snapped up three hundred Canadian working visas in a record forty minutes. The Spanish coast is flooded with refugees from Africa, most of whom live crammed into refugee camps. There's no place to go anymore. The Albanians have given up on Italy—there's no room since the Chinese hordes invaded. Highly-qualified Bulgarian

women work in Turkey as cleaners. The few remaining Austrian
elderly who can afford it hire highly-skilled caregivers from Slovakia. The Russians are making a big noise just about everywhere;
doing deals in Austria, living large in England, summering in Montenegro. Bulgarians once surged in the direction of Spain, yet now
they're in retreat, as if caught in a vicious undertow. The backwash
has caused of tidal wave of Bulgarian prostitutes to swamp Amsterdam. The red lights of Amsterdam's red light district now burn in
other parts of the city. During the day, fish, meat, and vegetables
are sold at the Albert Cuyp market, and at night, in the streets
parallel, red lights illuminate human flesh in shop front windows.

"It's terrible," says another acquaintance. "Have you heard that thing
about the earth opening up?" What do you mean by opening up?
I ask. "The earth just opens up, and then there are these gaping
holes that swallow everything in sight! It's happening everywhere,
in Guatemala, in China . . . Some guy in Florida had this hole open
up in the middle of his bedroom, and it swallowed him and his bed
together! We've had the same thing here at home, in Međimurje,
in Slavonski Brod, in Drniš. Didn't you hear about that guy from
Lovran? He was sitting on a bench on the promenade, and suddenly
a hole opened up in front of him. The guy and the bench went in
together!" my acquaintance shrieks, and then quietly adds: "I don't
know, I'd rather die of hunger than be swallowed up by a hole!"

In Europe it used to be only the Easterners who did the grumbling. Today everyone's at it. Easterners grumble because they didn't
get what they expected, and moreover, because everything they
ever worked for was sold for a pittance. Westerners grumble because their personal wealth has plateaued, and of course it's all the

Easterners' fault—whoever those damn Easterners are. Western Europe has been leveled by a tsunami of Easterners. Polish is the most frequently spoken language in England after English! C'mon, that can't be normal! . . . The reality is, Europe is a ruin; the continent littered with industrial skeletons, graveyards of progress, of communist and capitalist utopias alike. Europe is a twilight zone inhabited by losers, by "human remains," rats, drug addicts and alcoholics, prostitutes, the living dead, all furiously trying to end their own lives.

Europe is a circuit board for human flesh, travelers, traffickers, hucksters, migrants, new slave contingents, tourists, adventurers, believers, day laborers, pedophiles, pilgrims, pickpockets, drug dealers, undocumented workers, smugglers, murderers, tulip pickers and dish washers, street musicians and entertainers, the exploited and their exploiters. Everyone's on the make. People cry over old black-and-white images, their former lives seem a whole lot better. People cry watching National Geographic, moved by the deeply human lives of flora and fauna. People cry over clips of their past, suddenly seeing it in a completely different light. The threatening clatter of money has sent words once in general use into general hiding, or so people say. What words? Hope, dreams, passion, curiosity, the future, compassion . . . Today the only thing we hear, from all four corners of the globe, is a monotone rumbling drumming, hungry stomachs on the march. Tam-tam-tam-tam-tam-tam . . .

In the essay "Europe Today" (1935), Miroslav Krleža wrote that in Europe absolutely everything can be bought and sold, "and in place of the human being, money is today the only measure, the only scale, the only testimony to human virtue." Is money really the only measure of all things? "Europe—it's all about the *dengi*,

dengi, money, money," a taxi driver tells me as we glide the snowy streets of Oslo. He's Afghan. For some reason he's convinced I'm Russian, and so stutters away in Russian before translating himself into halting English.

Options still smolder in the dirt, but *the prisoners of starvation* are too exhausted to arise . . . *Debout, les damnés de la terre . . . Stand up, damned of the Earth . . . Ustajte prezreni na svijetu . . . Vstavaj, prokljat'em zaklejmennyj . . .*

2. A BOOK

A recent re-reading reading of Yuri Olesha's novel *Envy* provoked an equally disproportionate reaction in me as the old video clip did in my Zagreb acquaintance's husband. Olesha's short novel is what we might call "a great book." What makes a good book good, or a bad book bad, is a little easier to explain than what makes a book great. The books they hold dear say a lot about individual critics, reviewers, and other arbiters of literary values. In this respect, Nabokov's most personal book is that on Gogol. In his *Six Memos for the Next Millennium*, Italo Calvino outlined the six characteristics a book must bring together in order to become "great": lightness, quickness, exactitude, visibility, multiplicity, and consistency. *Envy* combines all six characteristics, yet even they don't fully explicate the greatness of Olesha's slender novel.

Canonic texts are not always reliable indicators of value; the protective embrace of the literary canon is often where thickest dust settles. Once it settles, literary kitsch fused with artistic mythologization is as hard to get rid of as dust. And who can be bothered jerking around making literary denunciations? It's an ungrateful job—canonization, like corruption, is something where there are many hands in the pie. Thankfully, by a kind of divine grace, some works establish standards of literary excellence under their own steam. Olesha's *Envy* is one of them.

Although the author of one of the more svelte oeuvres (a short novel, a handful of short stories, a play, a book of autobiographical sketches, a book for children and adults) within the general corpulence of Russian literature, Olesha is a shining light in the Russian avant-garde. *Envy* was published in 1927. Olesha obviously wasn't bothered by communism during its writing, and neither did communism have any qualms about publishing it. In the intervening years, nothing seems to have lessened its power. Down through the decades, it's as if a secret internal energy has kept the novel afloat, and it's as if this same energy catapulted it into the future, into our present; and that owing to this energy, it is today more brilliant, alive, and relevant than ever before.

What's the trick? Among the mythological anecdotes about Olesha there is one about him stopping by his publisher's office to collect his fee. The cashier refuses to hand it over because he hasn't got his ID on him.

"How can I pay you your fee when you don't have an ID? Tomorrow some other Olesha might show up with his hand out!"

Olesha, who was short in stature, straightened himself to his full height, and with magnificent tranquility replied: "There's no need to get worked up. If another Olesha ever appears, it'll be four hundred years before he comes along."

The trick, however, certainly isn't in the author's self-assurance. As in the aforementioned video clip, it's got more to do with the passing of time, the quality of distance. For my acquaintance's husband, the clip has the force of a surprise epiphany. The man—the one sitting at the computer in his Zagreb apartment, bawling his eyes out over banal images—is no mental patient. Like the majority of people, he's just a loser. And he might well have fallen straight out of Olesha's novel.

Envy consists of two parts: The narrator of the first part is Nikolai Kavalerov, a twenty-seven-year-old "loser," "poetic soul," and "nothing man." The second part is written in the third person, the novel's backbone formed by two antagonist characters, the two brothers, Andrei and Ivan Babichev. Andrei is a successful businessman, a man of the time, the time being that of the Soviet New Economic Policy. Ivan is a representative of the old, a "dreamer," "conjurer," "inventor," and a "drunk." Ivan is convinced that his brother Andrei has stolen his daughter Valya away from him, and that he now controls her. Together with Andrei and Valya, Volodya Makarov, a talented soccer player and Andrei's protégé, makes up the trio of representatives of the new time. Valya and Volodya are a successful young couple, the Soviet future. One night Andrei Babichev picks the drunk Nikolai Kavalerov up off the street and pityingly offers him a bed in his apartment until Volodya returns from a trip.

Kavalerov thinks his savior a monster: He is a man who "sings on the toilet" in the morning, a "glutton," a sausage maker, and big shot ("He, Andrei Petrovich Babichev, is director of the Food Industry Trust. He's a great sausage and pastry man and chef . . . And I, Nikolai Kavalerov, am his jester"). Andrei Babichev is a man who "lacks imagination," a man "in charge of everything that has to do with eating," he is "heavy, noisy, and by fits and starts, like a wild boar," and is both "greedy and jealous" ("He'd like to cook all the omelettes, pies, and cutlets, bake all the bread himself. He'd like to give birth to food. He did give birth to the Two Bits"). Kavalerov hates Andrei, and even when Andrei laughs, Kavalerov is fearful of him ("I listen, horrified. It's the laughter of a heathen priest. I listen like a blind man listening to a rocket explode"). Enormous and strong, Babichev has a terrifying physical presence, his head "like a painted clay bank."

Kavalerov (who, in spite of Olesha's efforts to avoid detection, is the author's alter ego) is characterized by his way of looking at the world. He sees the world from a bird's-eye perspective (and thus a cutter on the river is like a "gigantic almond cut lengthwise"); in the fragmented perspective of street mirrors ("I'm very fond of street mirrors. They pop up along your path. Your path is ordinary, calm—the usual city path, promising neither miracles nor visions. You're walking along, not assuming anything, you raise your eyes, and suddenly, for a moment, it's all clear to you: The world and its rules have undergone unprecedented changes"); through various poetic lenses; through movement, color, scent, sound, and half-closed eyes; he sees the world in metaphors, seeing the things no one else sees ("that man is surrounded by tiny inscriptions, a sprawling anthill of tiny inscriptions: on forks, spoons, saucers, his pince-nez frames, his buttons, and his pencils? No one notices them. They're waging a battle for survival"). Kavalerov observes the world through a "defamiliarized," "deautomaticizing," "deformed optic," so that a truck looks like a beetle "bashing around, rearing up and nosing down," cheeks like knees, a voice makes "the same sounds as an empty enema," a pair of glasses have "two blind, mercurially gleaming pince-nez disks," Anichka's face looks like "a hanging lock," her bed "like an organ."

Kavalerov is convinced that his life is a "dog's life." He scribbles "repertoire for showmen: monologues and couplets about tax inspectors, Soviet princesses, nepmen, and alimony," he'd like to be famous (somewhere in France), but knows that this is not his fate. Even "things don't like me. I'm hurting the street"; furniture "purposely sticks out its leg for me"; he even has a "complicated relationship" with his blanket—"a polished corner once literally bit me." Kavalerov is an envier, a Chaplinesque figure, a klutz, a coward, a doubting Thomas, a human "zero." Between the two opposites—the future embodied by his temporary "savior," Andrei Babichev, a successful NEP industrialist and sausage maker getting ready to feed the socialist world with a fast food chain named the Two Bits—and Ivan Babichev, a mad man, a fantasist, a trickster, the inventor of the *Ophelia* supper machine, a fabricator, and a prophet ("Who is he—Ivan. Who? A lazybones, a harmful, infectious man. He should be shot"), Kavalerov chooses the latter: "'My place is with him,' said Kavalerov. 'Teacher! I shall die with you!'"

This organizing typology is not new in Russian literature, there being clear antecedents in Russian Romanticism, in the figure of the educated, sensitive, and socially excluded hero (the so-called "superfluous man"), in the work of Pushkin and Lermontov, or in the heroes from the underground (Dostoevsky) who collide with the social apparatus. Goncharov's *Oblomov* provides the most direct antecedent of *Envy*'s oppositional pairing, its eponymous anti-hero a dreamer, a layabout, a loser who fears life itself. Oblomov's antagonistic other is Andrei Stoltz (the son of a Russian mother and German father), a practical, pragmatic, conscientious representative of the new time, a man of the future, and a man *for* the future. With Goncharov's novel, the term Oblomovism (*oblomovshchina*) entered the Russian lexicon of ideas as a synonym for slothfulness, for the

sensitive "Russian soul" who rejects rationalism, pragmatism, progress, and "the European West," whatever that was supposed to mean.
Yet there is a further parallel between Olesha's and Goncharov's
novels: Having retreated from life, Oblomov lives with the widow
Pshenitsina, while Kavalerov, it seems, will end his days sheltering
in the bed of the widow Anichka Prokopovich. The yellow pillow
that the false prophet Ivan Babichev carries about everywhere links
him with Oblomov, too. ("Tell him: Each of us wants to sleep on
his own pillow. Don't touch our pillows! Our still unfledged heads,
as rusty as chicken feathers, lay on these pillows, our kisses fell on
them in a night of love, we died on these—and the people we killed
died on them. . . . Here is a pillow. Our coat of arms. Our banner.")
The figure of the tragi-comic anti-hero, the weakling, the "poetic
soul" reappeared in the literature of the Russian avant-garde (e.g.
Ivan Bezdomny in Bulgakov's *Master and Margarita*), even smug-
gling itself into the literature of the seventies, as with Venichka, the
alcoholic in Venedikt Erofeev's *Moscow to the End of the Line*, the
emblematic figure. The pillow, like all symbols in Olesha's *Envy*,
also has a contrary meaning as a symbol of physical and moral fall
("and the pillow sat there next to him, like a pig"; "I would have
hurled myself into the terrible abyss, into the pillow's icy abyss").

It is as if the widow Prokopovich, with her impressive bed (which
her late husband won in the lottery), stands before the gates of hell.
She's "old, fat, and podgy" ("You could squeeze her out like liver-
wurst"), cooks for "a collective of hairdressers," and "goes around
entangled in animal guts and sinew" ("A knife flashes in her hand.
She tears through the guts with her elbows, like a princess tearing
through a spider's web"). Kavalerov's fall seems steeper still if we
remember his dream of wooing Valya, who "whooshed by . . . like

a branch full of leaves and flowers," who "will be washing up at the basin, shimmering like a carp, splashing, tickling the ivories of the water." (The description of Valya calls to mind Nabokov's Lolita.) Ivan Babichev is the opposite of his brother, their mutual hatred fierce. Andrei threatens Ivan with jail, and Ivan tells Andrei that he'll send his invention, the machine Ophelia, to kill him. Nothing of the sort actually happens: Andrei remains in the world of industrial fat cats (surrounded by his "adopted" children, Volodya and the beautiful Valya), and Ivan remains the self-declared "king of lowlifes." The successful remain on top; the people of the bottom, on bottom.

Ivan Babichev is one of the most memorable tricksters in European literature ("No charlatan from Germany— / Deceit is not my game. / I'm a modern-day magician / With a Soviet claim to fame!"). Ivan is a garrulous barfly, a kind of dilittante-Christ, whose miracles either miss their mark, or, according to legend, punish rather than heal. He's a drunk, a raconteur, in his self-description, a representative of "an epoch on the wane." The "steeds" and "elephants of revolution" are trampling his epoch underfoot, he a representative of the world of yesterday. ("That's me sitting on the pole, Andrysha, me, the old world, my era is sitting there. The mind of my era, Andrysha, which knew how to compose both songs and formulas. A mind full of dreams, which you want to destroy") Ivan, equally plausible as both Antichrist and pseudo-messiah, believes in his mission in the world. One such mission is to rouse "the bearers of decadent moods," those who feel "pity, tenderness, pride, jealousy," "all the emotions comprised by the soul of the man in the era now coming to a close"—and to warn them that they are doomed. Ivan finds an ally in Kavalerov and invites him to join the insurrection, advising that one should depart the stage of history "with a bang," that one should "raise one's fist to the coming world":

> "Yes, envy. Here a drama must unfold, one of those grandiose dramas in the theater of history that have inspired the lament, ecstasy, sympathy, and fury of mankind. Without even knowing it, you are a bearer of a historical mission. You are a clot, so to speak. A clot of envy in the dying era's bloodstream. The dying era envies the era that's coming to take its place."

> "What can I do?" asked Kavalerov.

> "My dear, here you must resign yourself or else . . . create a scandal. Go out with a bang. Slam the door, as they say. That's the most important part: go out with the bang. Leave a scar on history's ugly face. Shine, damn it! They aren't going to let you in anyway. Don't give up without a fight . . ."

Readers are generally able to identify with literary heroes, and their lines—whether those of Volodya Makarov, who wants to be a machine and considers that the understanding of time must become the chief human emotion, or those of Ivan Babichev (him being a prophet and all)—can form attractive manifestos. Olesha, however, rejects a world in which ultimate truth exists. And in "a world where there is no ultimate truth (a world without Christ), every option reveals itself to be incomplete, only partial. Ivan is the antipode of Andrei, yet also similar to him (he is contrary, but not contradictory, speaking the language of logic)."[1]

---

1   Igor Smirnov, "Roman i smena epoh: *Zavist* Jurija Oleshi," *Zvezda*, 8 (2012).

Great novels are like blotters, absorbing the fundamental dilemmas of their epochs while blindly anticipating future ones. Olesha's novel is one such blotter, functioning at multiple levels, uniting not only the richness of Russian literary history, but also that of West European literary history. The novel boldly calls up conflicts between the European giants, Rabelais and Cervantes, between biblical concepts (Adam, Jesus, the Antichrist), between avant-garde utopias (Volodya as man-machine) and socially utopian ideas and systems (revolution, communism, capitalism). Olesha draws the reader into a dramatic polemic of opposing concepts, yet nowhere does he offer final answers. Today, in a post-utopian time—when concepts flap around us like battered, moth-eaten flags, and when few still believe in the institutions of democracy, in the state, justice, equality, progress, the rule of law—we stand, each with our own pillow (whatever it might symbolize: security, home, a belief in family values), not knowing where to turn. We've tried all the options, and we've compromised the lot. And so we—like Kavalerov, who dithers over whether to sleep on a park bench or in the widow Anichka Prokopovich's bed—we dither between equally bad options in our own lives. To reach the bed, Kavalerov has to walk the stinking hallway where Anichka cooks soup from animal entrails ("Once I slipped on something's heart—small and tightly formed, like a chestnut"), meaning that in order to survive he has to embrace indifference—which is, in any case, what the prophet Ivan Babichev's new program encourages:

"I think that indifference is the best of all conditions of the human mind. Let's be indifferent, Kavalerov. Take a look! We've got ourselves a room, my friend. Drink. To indifference. Hurrah! To Anichka! And today, by the way . . . listen: I've got some good news for you . . . Today, Kavalerov, is your turn to sleep with Anichka. Hurrah!"

Like Kavalerov's, our resistance is feeble, and soon peters out. We're easily bought, which only sees our bitterness grow by the day. We can't make out the face of our enemy, or perhaps we simply don't want to see him. Perhaps that's why we constantly point the finger at others. Like Kavalerov, we're eaten by envy. We are the end of an era, unable to decipher the signs of what is coming. Our ability to imagine a new society has expired, and so we stand, like a blind man waiting expectantly for an explosion. We're caught in the same trap Olesha was in not even a century ago: "We know what was, we don't know what will be."[2]

3. AND YOU, WHERE DO YOU STAND?

Oh, yes, you're probably wondering how things turned out for my Zagreb acquaintance, the one who sent me the clip, and her husband. There's nothing much to tell. Her husband, thank Christ, finally quit bawling, and took matters into his own hands. How so? He took the taxi driver's exam, got his permit, and off he went. The children still haven't found jobs, so they sponge off her and her husband . . .

Oh, yes, what's the latest with my Zagreb acquaintance? Not much. Her husband ended up in the psych ward, they're going send him home soon, and then it's going to be tough, someone has to be with him, and she can't, because she works. She can't put him in care, a home costs more than double what she makes in a month. The kids are trying to go abroad, but that's tough too, their applications for Australian work visas were just rejected.

Oh, yes, what happened with my Zagreb acquaintance? Nothing much. She won the lottery. Not big money of course, but enough.

---

2   Ibid.

They bought a little piece of land, they're going to breed Californian earthworms, they even got an EU loan. And their son has started up a little business too. What kind of business? He's making fake ice cubes! How do they work? They're made out of plastic and go phosphorescent in the glass, but without cooling the contents, it's some sort of trick, people are crazy about them . . .

Oh, yeah, what happened with my Zagreb acquaintance? Nothing much. I'm trying to think up a happy ending, but it's not going so well. You've already worked it out—I'm with the losers. Nikolai Kavalerov is my brother ("I'm never going to be handsome or famous. I'm never going to come to the capital from a small town. I'm never going to be a commander, or a commissar, or a scholar, or a racer, or an adventurer"). Yes, I am his sister. Everything gives me away. I see the world through his eyes. I'm lazy like he is, envious like he is, and things don't like me either: The door handle is always catching my sleeve, the door always banging me on the snout. And like Kavalerov, I hate the high and mighty from the bottom of my soul. I'm drawn to snake-oil peddlers, conjurors like Ivan Babichev, slickers, street vendors hawking magical potions to eliminate stains, fire eaters and tub-thumpers, whom people avoid as if they were contagious, yet who only speak the prosaic truth. Oh yeah, I'm promiscuous, if one can put it that way. You can easily imagine me in bed with both Nikolai Kavalerov and Ivan Babichev—the old widow Anichka Prokopovich is in here too. The bed is enormous, joining with the horizon, we're all lying about—you've no idea how many we are! Oblomov's here, and Don Quixote, charging at pillows like they're windmills, Emma Bovary's here too, and Oskar Matzerath, and Molly Bloom, and Humbert Humbert, and Margarita, and Stephen Dedalus, and Tess d'Urberville . . . Many authors and their characters are here, and we're here too, their faithful readers, we're

all here, lying about on this enormous bed under a clear blue sky.
Our faces write a manifesto, bristling, unsettled, and shimmering
like a fish hatchery. We're on the bottom, and somewhere up high,
high above us rumbles time ("Then for the first time I heard the
rumble of time. Time was racing overhead. I swallowed ecstatic
tears," says Kavalerov), roars the modern world. Yet something tells
me that this bed full of losers, each clutching his or her pillow like
a life raft, will endure for a time to come, and that those above,
that they are ephemeral, like the sun and rain that cast a rainbow
above us, like the wind that blows golden leaves upon us, like the
snow that covers us like a duvet, and then melts . . . Of course,
one shouldn't believe in such things. Betting on the ephemerality of
those on the top, and the eternity of those on the bottom, is but the
sweet refuge of all losers. But then again . . .

By the way, though—you, where do you stand?

2.

MY OWN LITTLE MISSION

It's clear that everything is on its way to wrack and ruin, everything has been predetermined, there's no escape—you're going to perish, fat-nose! Every minute the humiliations are going to multiply, every day your enemy is going to flourish like a pampered youth. We're going to perish. That's clear. So dress up your demise, dress it up in fireworks. . . . Say farewell in such a way that your "goodbye" comes crashing down through the ages.

—*Yuri Olesha*, Envy

CIRCUS

EVERY DAY THE world we're living in is increasingly turning into . . . a circus. Yes, I know, the comparison's a dull one. It's what people used to say in ancient B.G. (Before Google). *It's a complete circus! My life has turned into a circus! Politics is a circus!* The word circus was an analogy for chaos, madness, unbecoming behavior, for events that had gotten out of hand, for life's more grotesque turns. It's possible, though, that the word might soon regain currency. Let's remember P. T. Barnum for a second, father of the circus and American millionaire, and his declaration that *no one ever went broke underestimating the intelligence of the American people.* Barnum's cynical declaration naturally doesn't only apply to Americans. The circus is global entertainment.

My next-door neighbor is in the habit of not taking his trash directly out to the big garbage bins on the street, preferring to leave them outside his front door for weeks. He dumps his wastepaper in a cardboard box, and when the wind blows it goes flying everywhere.

I can't work out why he finds it so hard to part with his trash, but I'm afraid to ask.

I spoke to the building superintendent.

"I'm afraid I can't help you. You know, lately people have become very *sensitive*," he said.

Sensitivity—there we go, another old-fashioned word. Really, every day people are more and more *sensitive*. Recently, a hypersensitive passerby elbowed me aside just because I was daydreaming and heading down the left and not the right side of the stairwell. Sensitivities vary, have various causes, and take various forms.

Some poor Dutchman bought a TV, but it turned out that it didn't work properly so he spent a year trying to sort things out. In the end, when his sensitivity hit overload, he packed a revolver and went back to the store where he bought the TV, with the obvious intent of shooting the boss. At the last minute he changed his mind and put a bullet in his own temple instead. Today even his children won't visit his grave, which is perhaps understandable. How do you honor the memory of a father who killed himself because of a television?

More recently, a twenty-six-year-old Tunisian, Mohamed Bouazizi, got all sensitive, lost his nerve, and set fire to himself on a main square somewhere in the Tunisian provinces. Since then heaps of stuff has happened, and a few more sensitive people have set themselves on fire. There was an Egyptian, then an Algerian . . . all in all, people have been catching fire like matchsticks.

In little Croatia, where out of sensitivity people punch each other's face in every now and then, a construction worker turned up on site and put a few rounds into his boss. Apparently he hadn't been paid in months. The media didn't show the slightest sensitivity toward his case.

And Đurđa Grozaj, she got all sensitive too. For thirty-five years the fifty-four-year-old single mother was employed in a Croatian clothing factory. Today the factory is in receivership and Đurđa is unemployed. Đurđa has joined the ranks of the aforementioned almost four hundred thousand unemployed. Together with her colleagues, as a sign of protest Đurđa went on a hunger strike. The public played the statue of the three monkeys. OK, well, not quite everyone. Đurđa and her colleagues were honored with the symbolic "Pride of Croatia" award and invited for coffee with the Croatian President. As she explained, that didn't mean much, because not having any money she'd already given up coffee. In December 2010, the bank decided to seize all Đurda's movable assets because of a debt of about seven hundred dollars. Đurđa had been a guarantor for a friend, who then didn't repay the loan, and so Đurđa made the repayments for as long as she could. The bank's writ was the straw that broke the camel's back, and Đurđa Grozaj decided to throw herself in front of a tram. The tram driver braked at the last minute. As she told reporters: "Even the tram didn't want to run me over."

Sensitivity, for better or for worse, isn't solely a human trait. Animals also display well-developed signs of sensitivity. At the same time the unfortunate Mohammed Bouazizi successfully self-immolated and Đurđa Groznaj unsuccessfully threw herself under a tram, dead birds fell from the sky all over the globe; in the city of Beebe, Arkansas, the Swedish town of Falköping, and in the Italian town of Faenza. On the English coast not far from Kent a heap of crabs washed up on the beach. Nobody's quite sure why. There's a kind of monkey (*Macaca fascicularis*), whose form of social organization is very similar to that of humans, which apparently has suicidal tendencies. Then there are claims that dogs often suffer from obsessive-compulsive disorder and have self-harm tendencies, like birds in cages that nervously pluck out their own feathers. The life of the sap-sucking insect known as the *Pea aphid*, parasitic on various forage crops, is also very sensitive. When attacked by ladybugs they're self-programmed to explode. Little suicide bombers.

Croats are yet to collectively give themselves up to suicide, although they've got all the reasons in the world why they should. The state is in complete collapse, people are hungry and depressed, and the government's been making asses of them for years. Croats, however, aren't united as a result of these major injustices suffered upon them, but because of the "injustice" suffered upon on a pair of Croatian generals at the war crimes tribunal for the former Yugoslavia in the Hague. A former Croatian president currently sitting in jail facing corruption charges, he's unusually sensitive too. He's constantly whining that his human rights and dignity have been violated. The government is also very sensitive at the minute. Over the past couple decades the ruling party has spent billions, not only on itself, but also on the defense of its criminals, and now it's steadfastly refusing to produce the receipts. That would be the fatal blow to its oh-so-sensitive dignity.

So, what to do, the circus has encircled us. Our lives are also a circus. What's more, it often seems that there's no exit to the tent. But whatever the case, sometimes one needs to pull one's socks up, head out to the park, sit on a lonely bench somewhere, open one's ears to the sweet song of the birds, and get down to reading a literary classic. A good book, they say, can save lives. I mean, Quirk Books, for example, offers an enviable range of classics, from *Android Karenina* to *Pride and Prejudice and Zombies*. They recently published Kafka's *The Meowmorphosis*, in which Gregor Samsa is transformed not into a giant bug, but into a cuddly little kitten. I'm sure the little kitten will warm your heart. With a sly grin on your face, just remember the millionaire P. T. Barnum, father of the circus, and his other reassuring declaration: *There's a sucker born every minute.*

FATAL ATRACTION

1.

An acquaintance of mine was into fly-fishing. I wouldn't have had a clue what it was all about had he not showed me his resplendent collection of flies, their miniature beauty enchanting. I could easily imagine a dazzled salmon in a shady Scottish stream, an alluring fly and jazzy feathers dancing before its eyes. Fly-fishing is a particularly expensive hobby. You can't just wade out into a Scottish stream willy-nilly wearing any old thing. Flies don't come cheap, either. But a gentleman is always willing to put his hand in his pocket for a spot of fishing. God knows how many times the money invested in the ritual exceeds the value of the fish caught. The satisfaction, quite obviously, isn't in the catching. Getting back to my acquaintance though, at some point his life changed and the accumulated years dulled his fly-fishing fervor. He packed on the pounds, his heart grew weak, and his spirit dissipated. All until recently. Out of the blue he got in touch while on a trip through Asia. He was with a guide fishing a pristine river in some kind of island jungle.

Fly-fishing had literally brought him back to life. The passions of others are the most mysterious things in the world.

2.

My acquaintance sent out his sudden electronic life beacon around the same time an online article caught my eye. A new consumer obsession has caught on among moneyed young men between the ages twenty-five and thirty-five. The majority of wealthy men in this age bracket are either soccer players or oligarchs. They're not spending their money on yachts, women, or art (bye-bye artists!) anymore, but on their sublimate—on aquariums. From Singapore to London a whole network of professionals has popped up to service this well-heeled clientele: aquarium designers and architects, underwater lighting experts, underwater gardeners for the aquarium ecosystem, suppliers of rare aquarium fish, ichthyologists, even fish therapists. Aquarium maintenance alone costs around a hundred and sixty thousand dollars annually. And aquarium fish are another matter entirely. At between eighty and two hundred thousand dollars a specimen, the platinum arowana is the most-highly priced, and prized. Its lack of pigment gives it a platinum-like color, making it a kind of albino among fishes, an apparent bearer of wealth and good fortune.[1] The platinum arowana is unusually sensitive, its optimal life expectancy around ten years. In order to test water quality, temperature, and a bunch of other water-related things, people put tester fish—known as "clown fish"—in first, the majority of whom die so that other fish may lead happy aquarium lives. "Clown fish" perform the role of slaves throughout history, offering

---

1   The belief that albino children bring bad luck lives on in parts of Africa. Every now and then a witchdoctor kills a pallid-looking child in order to prepare a voodoo potion. The child's organs are usually removed while he or she is still alive, so the child bleeds to death.

the same suicidal service, one akin to tasting whether the czar's, the emperor's, the king's, or the master's food has been poisoned.

The possible explanations for this trendy new obsession among flush young men are almost endless, and all are as right as they are wrong. The most straightforward can be found in language. In a number of languages, including a few Slavic languages, the equivalent of the word *chick* (i.e., an attractive young woman) is, believe it or not—*fish*. Is the aquarium a realization of the infantile dream of underwater worlds (and absolute control over them)? Or is it a symbolic substitute for a harem, one with "little sirens," with whom every touch is impossible and therefore all the more desirable? Or is it about a space of contemplation, a home temple in which the divine world swims around indifferent to the lives of mortals? Whatever the case, the fatal attraction between men and fish is fertile ground for psychoanalytical and other interpretive acrobatics.

3.

On the island of Kiribati the relationship between young girls, fish, and men is as clear as day. The Pacific Ocean feeds the world with fish, more than half the global tuna catch (two million tons a year) hauled up there. And it's not just European fishing fleets; Chinese, Taiwanese, Japanese, Russian, American, Thai, Indonesian, and Filipino boats are all there too. Kiribati waters swarm with fishermen and fish. From the age of twelve upward the little Kiribati girls slink around the fishing boats like cats. Prostitution isn't illegal on Kiribati. It's how the local girls earn a bit of pocket money to buy a few drinks, or get a few pounds of fish to feed their hungry families. The young prostitutes are called *korakorea* girls, *korakorea* meaning "cheap fish." The girls fall ill to venereal diseases, just like "clown fish" do from fishy ones. Here the reciprocal relationship between men and fish really is fatal.

4.

At the end of June this year I traveled via Vienna to Graz in Austria. The flight from Vienna to Graz was canceled so I had to take the bus. The young guy sitting next to me was a Russian from Ukraine, a soccer player, traveling to Graz for a two-day training camp.

"But why Graz? Aren't there any spare fields in Ukraine?"

The young guy shrugged his shoulders. Although he seemed to me barely seventeen, it turned out that Pavel was twenty-six, his club owned by a rich Ukrainian. A mafioso? A Ukrainian oligarch? No, no, a businessman, Pavel defended his boss.

"And how much do you earn?"

"Not much. Twenty thousand dollars a month."

In the world of major league soccer players, twenty thousand dollars a month is like beer money, Pavel explained. Pavel obviously wasn't interested in talking about soccer, or about oligarchs, or about his "wages," or about anything else for that matter.

"Tell me, is Vienna at the seaside?" he livened up.

"It's not."

"And Graz?"

"Graz isn't either."

Pavel quickly sunk into sleep. And while I looked at the sleeping boy on the seat next to me, a general sense of resignation came over me. He was on his way to Graz to train for a couple of days, and I was off to a literary evening. A barely literate Ukrainian was using his enviably nimble pair of legs to bring in twenty thousand dollars a month, while I, highly literate, for my "intellectual services" was bringing in incomparably less. With his monthly salary a soccer player like Pavel could buy four Hawaiian yellow tang, a popular aquarium fish, at five thousand dollars a pop. Pavel might be barely literate, but as opposed to me, he was born with an innate knowledge. He knows all too well that he's only a little fish in the aquarium. He knows he's replaceable, and that he only costs his boss one, two, or three platinum arowanas (the price of which has apparently fallen lately) a year. I on the other hand, who drank "arrogant" ideas about the rights of all to equality with my socialist milk, haven't been able to shake the thought that I'm irreplaceable, although the wages that await me in Graz for the provision of intellectual services equal a portion of fried sardines. In a better restaurant, of course. Yes, I am a *korakorea*-girl, a cheap fish. And with that thought for comfort, and my young fellow passenger having mistaken my shoulder for a pillow, I too sink into sleep.

BAD PUPILS

A glance at the faces of those who in this society are someone can help understand the joy of being no one.

(*The Invisible Committee,* The Coming Insurrection)

I'M SITTING IN a Zagreb café and, as is my custom, I'm eavesdropping. Spying on the everyday is half a writer's job; the rest is creative filtering of the information gleaned. Maxim Gorky would be happy to hear that. And in any case, it's more than time we gave a thought to the unjustly loathed classics of socialist realism.

There are two girls at the table next to mine. One is like a rocket: taut, firm jaw, cleavage pumped out, aerodynamic. The other is like pudding: soft, stoop-shouldered, down in the mouth . . .

"Every morning I make myself a juice and eat a plate of cereal. I mean, sometimes it happens that I nibble on this or that too, but I don't start the day without juice and cereal. No way!" says rocket-girl.

"Really?" asks the other, enchanted.

"For me it's written in stone. And when you write something in stone, there's no way anyone's gonna get one over you."

"Truly?"

"I was at my pedicurist's the other day, and the chick says to me, hey, how about I round your nails off a little, those straight ones of yours are so out. Not a chance, I tell her. Why, she asks, they'd look better on you. I know what looks best on me. Where would I be if I didn't know that?!"

"On one hand you'd have round nails, and on the other you'd have straight ones," says pudding-girl timidly.

"You know what I'm saying?"

And while I listen to the self-confident girl, she who is incapable of being thrown off track, it occurs to me that Maxim Gorky and his slogan "Humankind—how proud that sounds!" are to blame. In time the slogan won over a good part of the world. This big idea about the pride of humankind was adopted by democratic societies, parents, psychoanalysts and psychotherapists, self-help gurus and trainers, priests and thieves, children and killers with children's faces, politicians and voters, bankers and traders, spin doctors and the kindlers of human self-confidence, and—look at that—we all entered a new time as a result. We all have the right to happiness, we can do anything (anything we want), we all have our opinions, we all know what we want, and we deserve to have it all. *Self-confidence, self-worth, self-respect, self-integrity, self-regard*—they're all ladders to climb on the road to success. Doubting oneself, whether it's low self-esteem or procrastination, has been declared a dysfunction, perfectionists are mental patients, contemplation a deferral of action. Even the Wikipedia entry on procrastination is accompanied by an image of Rodin's *The Thinker*. Thinkers are dysfunctional persons in need of expert help.

What has happened to society as a consequence? While murderers murder, procrastinators dilly-dally about whether to pull the trigger.

While good artists spend time getting intimate with their doubts, the bad take over the galleries. While good directors lose their minds working on film, the films of the bad flood the cinemas. While serious scholars are blocked by "academic procrastination," the bad storm the department. While good pop and rock musicians inevitably die young, the bad haunt the stage well into their eighties. While good journalists spend time studiously researching the facts, the bad usurp their places by selling lies. While the rare honest politician is wracked with doubts, the irresponsible govern without a care in the world.

There's a video clip on YouTube that functions as a visual metaphor of the society of spectacle at its peak. In the clip, Russian President Vladimir Putin struggles to bang out a few notes on the piano, and then sings the old standard, *Blueberry Hill*. It's painfully bad. America's finest musicians accompany Putin's performance, and out front, in the audience, the country's entertainment elite rises to its feet. Famous actors and actresses mouth the words and sway in rhythm, all in a show of support for Putin. Putin is a child with worryingly high self-confidence, the actors and actresses parents lovingly watching their progeny.

An innocent joke remains lodged in my memory from the time of Yugoslav communism, coincidentally the only joke in circulation immediately following Tito's death. A father catches his son smoking the crappy local *Drava* cigarettes.

"Bad cigarettes are dangerous for your health, here's some money, go buy yourself those expensive Marlboros."

The next day the father catches his son swigging hooch.

"Hooch wrecks your liver, here's some money, go buy Johnnie Walker."

The third day the father catches his son reading *Start*, a local lads' magazine.

"Don't waste your time, here's some money, go buy *Playboy*." A short time later, the kid asks his father excitedly:

"Dad, who gets to sleep with the playmates?"

"The best in the class, my boy, the best in the class!"

Let's rewind the tape. The father said: The best in the class. And until society rehabilitates the father from the joke and his message that only the best in the class win the right to advancement, the world will continue its slide toward its—beginnings. Because bad pupils have gained control over all of us. They're who we vote for, who we listen to; they're all we see. Bad pupils have usurped the government, political forums, and the media; they produce the food we eat and the drinks we drink; they design our clothes and our surroundings. Bad pupils color our mental landscape; they're the teachers in our schools, they write the books we devour. Bad pupils are our media idols, establishing the values we accept as our own, modeling us to their standards. Bad pupils employ us, determining the amount we are paid—they are our lords. And lorded over by bad pupils, we're all gradually becoming dunces. That's why governments are so happy to cut education funding.

A little rake with an outstretched hand approaches the table next to mine. Rocket-girl takes a note from her handbag and gives the kid twenty kuna.

"Isn't that a bit much?" pudding girls inquiries.

The kid vanishes.

"And a thank you?!" rocket-girl yells after him. "Jesus, have you noticed how many beggars there are in Zagreb lately?!"

Pudding-girl is silent.

"Before it was just the gypsies. Now everyone's got their hand out," says rocket-girl, frowning with worry.

Taking a cigarette from the packet on the table, she lights up and lets out a long drag.

LIQUID
TIMES

A BICYCLE-EYE view is a view out on the world. When you ride a bike your gaze doesn't linger long on your surroundings, but neither does the world exactly flash by, particularly when you ride as leisurely as I do. The elevated position and nonchalant circling of the pedals allows you register things, but doesn't give you time for empathy. Here I need to add that the view out from my bike is always of the same restricted space, of a park in my Amsterdam neighborhood.

The park has changed a lot over the past decade, it's a long while since it was a space for urban escapism. Today, particularly on the weekends, it's crawling with joggers, cyclists, and walkers of all ages and nationalities. Before you'd only see young men out jogging, now you see tubby middle-aged women wrapped in hijabs. People used to cruise around on their bikes. Today, little mobility scooters barrel down the bike paths, unruly old folk at the steering wheel. Sometimes you even see an entire Turkish brood heading off to do the shopping on them. Then there are the kids on Vespas, the invalids in their wheelchairs, and the increasingly wary cyclists.

My gaze settles on a small posse bounding toward me. There's a young man chugging along pushing a twin-size baby stroller. A young woman with a boy in tow follows close behind. A girl and a dog bring up the rear. This family out for a morning jog would be fantastic material for a pro-life propaganda video, that's if—dog and baby twins excepted—they weren't all clenching their jaws. There isn't the slightest trace of pleasure on their faces. They might as well have stayed home and cleaned their teeth.

Actually, no one's cheerful anymore. Not the scowling old fellow, plastic bag in one hand, grumpily hurling clumps of dry bread into the lake with the other. Not the young couple with a child who's watching the angry old boy, and not the teenager sauntering past totally indifferent. It's a sunny Saturday morning, little sailboats and winsome ducks gently glide across the lake. The trees and grass exude a calming shade of green. So why the general anxiety dimming the glow of this Amsterdam park life idyll?

According to demographers and the newspapers, life on earth is getting a little crowded. The number of earthlings has just topped seven billion. India, currently with a population of around 1.2 billion is soon to overtake China as the most populous country on earth. The developed countries of today are projected to experience future depopulation, while developing countries such as Nigeria are expected to see population explosions. Some 1.5 billion earthlings live on less than a dollar a day, and huge numbers perish from hunger. People with a planetary view of the world are worriedly wondering if in the near future we'll all be hungry, and whether there aren't simply too many of us. Perhaps this accounts for why more and more people are asking themselves how to die. I mean, when there's no answer to the question of how to live.

Demographers suggest that the demographic picture of little Croatia is currently in a bad way. More people are dying than being born, and Croats no longer believe in church or state. The raging procreational passion that erupted with the birth of the Croatian state has long since fizzled. These days, potential parents don't have jobs and so live with their parents, not in any position to rent, let alone buy an apartment. And they're a curse on the homes of their parents, who themselves are barely surviving on miserable pensions. Unofficial statistics suggest than every second Croat is a thief. This dirty little detail helps sap the procreational impulses of potential parents. It also helps explain why young Croatian women down contraceptive pills like sedatives.

But even death is an expensive solution. The price of cemetery plots has gone through the roof. With thieves, gangsters, murderers, and politicians all desperate for their deeds to outlive their mortal coils, there's a mad scramble on for prime plots at Zagreb's main cemetery. The Catholic Church in Croatia granted (not without a fee of course) deceased Croatian president Franjo Tuđman pole position at the very entrance, where hitherto there had only been a chapel. Today, Tuđman's majestic grave stands almost buttressed behind the chapel, the new layout like a symbolic sentry box surveilling the entire cemetery. In this new order of things it's immediately clear who rules the Croatian dead, present and future. Tuđman's devotees among the living quickly started scrapping for the first row. The heirs to old graves never dreamed of selling out their great-grandmothers' and fathers' final resting places. But the ambitious buyers are generous to a fault, which is understandable. They're buying a spot in the eternal gallery. And in this respect a new social order is taking form in the graveyard. Wealthy dead folk squeeze out poor dead folk.

"Resomation" or "green cremation" is a new invention in corpse management, a natural process for the speedy decomposition of the body. The deceased is fed into something called a "resomator" (which looks like an elongated washing-machine) and at high pressure exposed to a water and potassium hydroxide solution. After three hours the machine spits back out around 200 gallons of mineral-rich liquid. Dental implants, crowns, pacemakers (which don't explode like they do during cremation!) and other remains are ground into a fine ash and given to the family, the volume of ash being much less than that remaining after cremation. Resomation also consumes eight times less energy. The deceased's liquid remains can be used as fertilizer, or just tipped down the sink. The process even erases any DNA trace of the deceased's identity.

Resomation is currently legal in a handful of American states and several European countries. The Scots, incidentally, have the patent on resomation. Given the lack of cemetery space in Switzerland, resomation might soon be the only available burial option. And those who care about the environment can breath easy: Resomation is eco-friendly. "We are all dust and it is to dust we shall return" could soon be: "We are all liquid and it is as liquid we shall end." For the many people who felt their lives worthless, posthumous transformation into this truly liquid form could be of some comfort (*Water the lettuce with Grandma! We've never had such tasty lettuce before! Spray the geraniums with Granddad!*)

What happens to the soul in the process of resomation—whether our soul is hydrophobic or water-resistant; whether on hitting the water it turns into a little submarine and rides the storm, or simply dissolves; whether at high pressure it is catapulted into the air like a miniature rocket, or simply evaporates—these are questions best left to wise men of theology. One thing is certain: Zygmunt Bauman is right. We live in a liquid era.

JUMPING OFF
THE BRIDGE

I **WAS GLUED** to reports on the recent riots in the London boroughs of Tottenham, Hackney, and Brixton, stunned by the images of seething youth smashing shop windows and making their grab for street wear and electronics. Expensive mobile phones apparently topped their consumer desires, a detail that disappointed many commentators (*If only they'd stolen bread and milk we'd understand!*). I became fixated on something else though: A Waterstones bookstore the kids passed by might as well have been an undertaker's. But they didn't miss a beat in cleaning out the backpack of another dazed and confused kid who obviously needed medical attention, leaving him bloodied and lost in the street. On our television screens, shocked, we all saw what we wanted to see. Each of us projected our own fears onto the Rorscharchian stain of the London riots.

Around the same time, the beginning of August 2011, a Serbian news portal carried a witty article about the opening of a new bridge. In Belgrade, the capital, there's an old bridge called Branko's Bridge. Although named after the Serbian poet Branko Radičević, it's better known for the fact that another Branko jumped from it, Branko Ćopić, a fellow writer. The author of the article noted that among terminally morose Serbian writers, the opening of the new bridge had been greeted with rare delight, and that a kind of competition was on to see who'd christen the bridge with a jump, thus winning naming rights. The bookies were already taking bets on the next writer-suicide. Among the many comments on the article, someone made an appeal that these things not be joked about; someone else observed that others might also like to think about jumping (*Why only writers? What about single mothers?*); a third person suggested that politicians should take a jump (*Jump Tadić![1] We'll call it Boris's Bridge, for sure!*); a fourth person remarked that a lot of people in Serbia unfortunately seemed to have no idea who Branko Ćopić was; a fifth suggested that a list of candidates for pushing be prepared.

Why did I single out this particular episode? I could have equally mentioned Anders Breivik, the Norwegian "anti-Islamic crusader," who just a few days previously had killed seventy-seven people, the majority of them teenagers. Or the band of thieves who robbed a handful of people in a Budapest suburb and then buried them alive in a nearby forest. Or the story of a pack of Zagreb hooligans who bashed a pair of French tourists simply because the pair refused to buy them a round of drinks. I could have mentioned falls on the stock exchange, the soaring Swiss franc, the global recession, and the bankers impunibly running the show. I could have brought up the numerous demonstrations against "the swine of capitalism," the messages of which haven't reached the pudgy ears of those with

---

1   A reference to Boris Tadić, president of Serbia at the time.

their snouts deepest in the trough. Because all of this, and a lot of other stuff too, happened within more or less the same timeframe.

The devastating fact is that the majority of the young English rioters were barely literate. The research and the terrifying statistics are there. The reading ability of sixty-three percent of fourteen-year-old boys from the white working class, and more than fifty percent of their Afro-Caribbean peers, is at the level of the average seven-year-old. The majority of these kids leave school and continue their education on the streets. "Other kids go from school to university. We go from school to prison," said one of them. Their "girlfriends" get pregnant early. In comparison with other European countries, Great Britain has the highest rate of teenage pregnancy. At best semi-literate, left to their own devices, and with few chances of finding any kind of job, these kids form an angry, disenfranchised mass whose futures have been stolen. They have absolutely no reason to believe in social institutions, and vandalism is the only means of articulating their fury. "I didn't want this kind of life. It just happened to me," said one boy.

The image of the life they desired is one that their society served them up as desirable (*I want to be rich, I want lots of money / I don't care about clever, I don't care about funny*). In an ideological package such as this, the system of values in operation in everyday life doesn't assume literacy, education, responsibility, or work (*Life's about film stars and less about mothers / It's all about fast cars and cussing each other*). That's why confronting one's own loser status is, for all intents and purposes, just another form of self-deceit (*But it doesn't matter cause I'm packing plastic / and that's what makes my life so fucking fantastic*), in exactly the same way that vandalism is a mute form of conceding one's own defeat (*And I am a weapon of massive consumption / And it's not my fault it's how I'm programmed to function*).

Years have passed since the clearing of the utopian fog and the fall of the Berlin Wall. In spite of the many warnings, the piles of books written sounding the alarm, the multitude of demonstrations that have pointed to ever-increasing social stratification, in spite of institutional and extra-institutional attempts to resolve or attenuate the worst of the consequences, society, deaf and blind, has marched on. In the meantime grandmothers and grandfathers, those who lived with full faith in the system, have gone into hard-earned retirement and then died of hunger. In the meantime their children have had children and discovered with horror that they aren't in a position to support either themselves, or their children. In the meantime, their children have also had children, the penny dropping that their futures have no future. And in the meantime, a heaving mass has been born, a tribe of millions, déclassé and inured, incapable of remedying their position, because they don't know who their real enemy is anymore. All their lives they've had it drilled into them that it all comes down to their personal choices and individual ability. And today, looking at its "feral" children, society, stupefied by the mantras of democracy and free choice, continues to try and convince these kids that they're cutting off the branch on which they're sitting. They might be barely literate, but the children know that the branch has been rotten for years, and can't hold their weight in any case. The only weapon they possess is their rage.

And I, who by all accounts should be on the opposite side, am at this very moment much closer to these kids than any of them could imagine, and much more than I would have ever imagined. I didn't want this kind of life either, but there you go, it happened to me. If nothing else, the kids and I are bound—by fear (*I don't know what's right and what's real anymore / I don't know how I'm meant to feel anymore / When do you think it will all become clear? / 'Cause I'm being taken over by the fear*).

And while day and night I flagellate myself with the news, while my heart pounds like a beat-up dog cowering against a wall, I extinguish my fears with fantasies about them, about the kids who will soon (yes, soon!) in their millions crawl from their ghettoes, and fists raised descend on Wall Street, or wherever they're needed. My fantasies, however, don't hold out for long, and soon burst like a polychrome bunch of birthday balloons. (*Forget about guns and forget ammunition / 'Cause I'm killing them all on my own little mission / Now I'm not a saint but I'm not a sinner / Now everything's cool as long as I'm getting thinner*).[2]

And as far as jumping off the bridge goes, good taste keeps me from being so predictable. I'm not going jump, no way! Unless it makes me thinner. And if it does, then it's goodbye, Weight Watchers! Hello, Revolution!

---

2 All cited lyrics are from Lily Allen's "The Fear."

A
MOUTHFUL

Who's there?
Hunger!
Ooh, hunger!
("Money," Cabaret)

BLESSED WERE THE times of totalitarian dictatorships and information blockades! Today, thanks to the information revolution, barely a day goes by without a disturbing piece of news unnerving me. If every revolution eats its children, then this one, the information revolution, is the bloodiest of all. I mean, who ever really knew what a tsunami was, let alone had heard of the region where it hit?! In the old days, who knew who had mugged and robbed whom? These kinds of stories nibble away at my hard won reserves of internal peace. In communist dictatorships people lived longer and healthier lives. Promised a brighter future, many were convinced they'd live to see its dawn. The reality is that excessive information exposure is more harmful than radiation. The fall of communism, globalization, the incontestable hegemony of capitalism, and Francis Fukuyama with his end of history have ruined the health of millions.

Bubba, my countryman, spends most of his day voluntarily hooked up to every available source of information. Bubba's daily phone calls raise my drowsy consciousness to a state of emergency.

"Hello, you there? Get yourself to the bank, quick."

"Why?"

"Withdraw the lot."

"There's nothing to withdraw."

"Christ, you must have something!?"

"Loose change."

"Take it out!"

"But why?"

"Buy provisions."

"What kind of provisions?"

"You know, food."

"What kind of food?"

"Flour, oil, tinned stuff, dough, zwieback, definitely zwieback . . . Didn't you ever do the weekly shopping with your mom?!"

Actually, I do remember. On the first of the month Dad would fetch a canvas satchel and we'd all go grocery shopping together. Mom would buy just enough to see us through to the next payday: oil, flour, rice, pasta. Mom's pantry was a place of wonder: lined up in neat orderly rows were jars of preserves, jams, pickles, paprika, beetroot, sacks of potatoes, small casks of sauerkraut, smoked bacon, crackling, and ham, jars of lard and honey, little boxes of cookies . . .

"Don't forget the garlic."

"Why garlic?!"

"In case of riots and a police crackdown."

"What's garlic got to do with the police?!"

"If you're out and about and there's a riot you can rub the garlic into a scarf and cover your mouth and nose. Garlic's great against tear gas."

"What are you on about?"

"Buy batteries, a transistor radio, a torch, a pocketknife, and a few essentials from the local camping store."

"But why?!"

"Haven't you heard of nine meals from anarchy?"

The phrase "nine meals from anarchy" was apparently coined by Lord Cameron of Dillington in the hope of rousing shopping drunk British consumers from their slumber. Let's imagine, for instance, that one day there's no petrol at the pump. Trucks wouldn't be able to make their daily food deliveries to the supermarket. And given that almost no one keeps provisions at home, it's estimated that the food on supermarket shelves would go in three days. At three meals a day, we'd only have nine meals before total anarchy. Things are, of course, much more complex. It's a matter of chain reactions. Every increase in the price of petrol increases food production costs, and increased production costs increase the price of the product. Chaos would ensue if cash machines crashed for a day. Nobody keeps cash at home anymore. But things are, of course, much more complicated still. Today the crisis is all pervasive, and unemployment is all pervasive, and this means that hunger is crouching at the door of millions of people—those who don't have the faintest idea what hunger is. Because until now hunger has always been somewhere else. On television reports of starving African children covered in burly flies.

A few years ago I was in Sofia, Bulgaria. The acquaintance I was staying with lived downtown in a typical East European apartment block. Thirty years ago they were pretty apartments, that much is apparent from the spaciousness and the detailing. The apartment was now in a desperate state of disrepair. We went out onto the balcony for a cigarette. On the neighboring balcony I noticed an unusual wire contraption.

"What's that?"

"Ah, that's our ingenious neighbor," said my acquaintance. "He hunts pigeons with it. He made it himself."

"What does he want with pigeons?"

My acquaintance laughed tartly and shrugged her shoulders.

"A lot of people are struggling here . . ." she said.

It's been a few years since that conversation on the Sofia balcony, but at this very moment I remember that resourceful Bulgarian with respect. Things have changed in the space of several years. Even I've wised up recently, in every respect. I've honed my consumer instincts, and for the first time in my life I've started comparing prices and am more than willing to travel a little farther if it means saving a few pennies. I recently bought a load of Dutch cans of condensed milk at about a dollar and a quarter a can. The cans are identical to the old Soviet ones, Russians called the contents *zguschenka*. From a single can of *zguschenka* you could make a liter of milk. As opposed to the Dutch cans, the Russian cans didn't have an expiry date, edible for eternity.

And as far as pigeons go, I'm resolute there: no way, ever. Pigeons are plain revolting.

"You're right," says Bubba. "Set limits. It doesn't matter how hungry you are, don't ever ingest what revolts you."

Thank God I've got a copy of the Croatian translation of the famous *Apicius* cookbook. Flamingo was one of the greatest delicacies on the ancient Roman table and luckily Amsterdam Zoo is full of the elegant pink birds. Flamingo needs to be boiled a little first, then

you flavor it with spices, douse it with white wine, and put it in the
oven. Pheasant doesn't hold a candle to flamingo.

Amsterdam's parks are hopping with hundreds of thousands of
rabbits, and numerous flocks of plumpish ducks paddle the canals.
For now, it seems, there's no reason for concern. The Dutch were
long kind to immigrants. They're not anymore. But there are some
exceedingly cunning fauna that manage to flout the strict legal controls, sneaking their way in undocumented. That's what happened
a year or so ago when, tired of the long south-north flight, a gaggle
of Egyptian geese landed on Dutch soil and decided to set up camp.
The feathery Egyptian felons would have gone unnoticed had a few
articles not appeared in the tabloids about how these brawny Egyptian geese were threatening their autochthonous counterparts with
extinction. I've got no idea what an autochthonous Dutch goose
looks like, but I've clocked the Egyptian geese sauntering around
the neighborhood tram stop. Egyptian geese are unusually chunky,
so as you approach the tramlines it's as if there are big clumps of
snow lying there. Yes, things have changed: Today immigrants are
good to the Dutch.

Like I said, I've honed my instincts. I run the scenarios in my head.
I've got a Plan B up my sleeve and a Plan C under development.
Apart from the kidnapped flamingos, rabbits, and ducks of unidentified origin, and renegade Egyptian geese, lately I've been eyeing
up my Chinese next-door neighbor. He's youthful, compact, short-
ish, has supple joints, toned, tanned calves (he wears shorts in the
summer!), a cute face and smooth skin. My Dutch neighbor on the
other side I don't even give a second look: He's my age, gone to
seed, has big ashy eyelids and an unhealthy complexion. All in all,
more sausage than steak.

SOUL
FOR RENT!

I think it's just elegant to have an imagination, I just have no imagination at all. I have lots of other things, but I have no imagination.
(*Marilyn Monroe,* The Seven Year Itch*)*

SHORTLY BEFORE THE whole world slid into financial crisis a Dutchman, the head of some kind of association, contacted me explaining that he was a fan of my books, and that he'd like to organize a literary evening.

"And you'd be the moderator?"

"Yes."

"You're a literary critic?"

"No, I'm a physical education teacher."

"So you're into sports then?"

"No, cultural exchange."

"And where would the literary evening be?"

"In Poland."

"Where exactly?"

The Dutchman mentioned the name of a village. As it turned out the Dutchman had a holiday home there, where he spends most of the year. Other Dutch also had houses in the village. Then it came out that the physical education teacher actually organized group tours for Dutch tourists, accompanying them around the surrounding countryside and introducing them to authentic Polish village life. His mission wasn't just to enlighten Dutch tourists about Polish culture, it was also about enriching the everyday lives of the local population. I was supposed to be the enrichment. The physical education teacher's benevolent enterprise had already received accreditation for its innovative embrace of European integration.

"Who are you accredited by?"

"European Union agencies. We get some funding from them, the rest comes from membership dues."

"And this is how you earn a living?"

"One has live from something," he said meekly.

Irrespective of the fact that I was and remain wholeheartedly in favor of initiatives supporting European integration, not to mention intercultural communication, I declined the invitation, which only goes to prove my arrogance and worrying deficit of visionary imagination. Let me repeat: This was all before the crisis. Today I'd no doubt be more receptive to the offer.

Yes, we live in a time of crisis. Many are thinking about means of survival, yet most suffer failures of imagination. For example, in Croatia a couple of middle-aged women (one of whom was educated as a political scientist) went to jail after botching a bank robbery. For my part, I appreciate an imaginative approach. I think it's elegant when someone, even in times of crisis, has an imagination. Perhaps I have lots of other things, but I have no imagination.

That's why I was thrilled to read about a little Croatian start-up. Buying pigs' ears from a local slaughterhouse (cheap, of course—pig's ears rarely make it onto anyone's menu), a guy figured he could grind them into prime dog food. Crisis or not, there are plenty of buyers. People obviously figure that even if their own lives aren't up to much, they can at least try and give their pets a decent one.

I was equally taken by the example of well-known gourmet chef, Daniel Angerer, and his wife. The pair had a young baby, and in case her milk dried up the wife put some away in reserve. With the fridge soon overflowing with breast milk, the pair decided to make cheese from it. Angerer launched the new venture by approaching volunteer tasters with little cheese, fig, and pepper sandwiches. Many turned up their noses. Angerer's wife maintained that the prevailing skepticism toward mother's milk cheese stems from the fact that most people "associate breasts with sex," instead of accepting the fact that "women's breasts exist to produce food."

Angerer's idea was taken up by artist Miriam Simun in the installation *The Lady Cheese Shop*. Visitors were offered breast milk cheese, the goal being to examine "the relationship between ethics and modern biotechnology." London restaurateur Matt O'Connor has a dish called "Baby Gaga" on his menu, breast milk ice cream. It's around twenty-two dollars a portion. O'Connor maintains that "no one's done anything interesting with ice cream in the last hundred years," and pays his donors well. One wet nurse shyly explained that given she has excess milk, the extra income was very welcome in these recessionary times. The woman is right. If people sell their kidneys, blood, and children to survive, why wouldn't women sell their milk. I mean, if they've got it to spare.

Some people's imaginations really take the cake. It isn't just breast milk that brings in the punters, nostalgia works a treat too.

Lithuanians, for example, figured out that there was a dollar to be made in commercializing their traumas under the terrors of Soviet communism. As part of the project *1984: Survival Drama in a Soviet Bunker*, visitors crawl down into an authentic six-meter deep Soviet bunker in a Lithuanian forest somewhere, exposing themselves to the risk of physical and mental torment. Visitors are happy to put their hands in their pockets to hear (for a first or second time) Soviet guards yelling: "Welcome to the Soviet Union! Here you are nobody and nothing!"

Hungarian director Péter Bacsó's 1969 film *The Witness* (*A tanú*) features a communist amusement park. There's a scene in a funhouse in which Marx's, Lenin's, and Stalin's heads leap out of the darkness, prompting general shrieking in the audience. The scene inscribed the film in the memories of my generation as a brilliant and emancipatory satire on the absurdities of communism. Of course the film itself spent some time in a bunker, and is today almost forgotten. After the fall of the Berlin Wall, communist theme parks have sprung up in a number of post-communist countries, but as there's no risk, they're no longer entertaining, and least of all emancipating. Viliumas Malinauskas is a wealthy Lithuanian farmer (mushrooms and snails) and the owner of Grūtas Park, a sculpture garden located in a forest next to the village of the same name, the park home to socialist realist statues scavenged from the ruins of Lithuanian communism. Visitors can have their photo taken in the embrace of tons of bronze—Stalin, Lenin, Marx, and Engels are all there—or if they prefer, with living sculptures, performance artists impersonating the same crew. In Lithuania, a land of Catholicism and former communism, a battle for market share is raging. It remains to be seen whether dead communism or living Catholicism will win the day.

Incidentally, let's not forget that from a commercial perspective, communism still appears to sell amazingly well in the country of its former rival, America. Every now and then a new literary star emerges from the undergrowth to testify about his or her communist trauma due to lack of bananas and toilet paper. The reality is that these stars are getting younger and younger (and cuter and cuter!), so can't have had any real personal contact with communism in the first place. But yeah, genes and a place of birth are always solid guarantees of purported authenticity. The marketplace knows that the inauthentic recycling of trauma always sells better than authentic experience from first-hand.

Some people really do have great imaginations. The London culinary expert assured us that there had been nothing new in the ice cream world for the past hundred years. But there's no way that's the case with tourism, where they're innovating on a daily basis. Hence the appearance of so-called *dark tourism* and its specific sub-genres. There's *grief tourism* (tourists visit concentration camps, infamous prisons, historic graveyards, battle sites of mass slaughter, or the small town of Soham, England, where two ten-year-old girls were once killed); *disaster tourism* (tourists visit places struck by natural catastrophes, post-Katrina New Orleans, post-tsunami Thailand, etc.); then there's *poverty tourism* (tourists visit infamous shanty towns such as Soweto in South Africa, or the favela of Rio de Janeiro); and then there's *doomsday tourism* (tourists go to places threatened with disappearance, the Galápagos Islands, Greenland, tiny coral islands such as Great Barrier Reef in Australia).

The newest branch of tourism on offer is *political tourism*. It's all about educational visits to political hotspots. Tour operators organize both group and individual trips to countries such as Turkey, Georgia, North Korea, Northern Ireland, Ethiopia, Kosovo, and Bosnia. The tour guides are always experts, acclaimed historians, diplomats, academics, respected commentators, and journalists. The clients are whoever is prepared to pay. The cost of an eight-day trip to Bosnia is just over four thousand dollars. The tour is led by a well-known British journalist and involves meetings with local politicians, NGOs, religious leaders, regular people, and authentic victims of the Bosnian war. Surviving victims, naturally.

For many of these troubled hotspots, the potential windfall from political tourism could be a saving grace. The Balkans has a lot to offer. It's perhaps only a matter of time before ethnic cleansing and detention camps inspire theme parks. Tourists could get their ethnic chips (Serb, Croat, Bosnian, Albanian, etc.) with their entry tickets and then chase each other around the park ethnically cleansing one another. Communism could be a starter too. Goli otok, the Yugoslav gulag, has a mild Mediterranean climate, and given its accessibility, incomparably better tourist potential than Siberian camps. In short, if there's a growth market for anything in the states that have sprouted from the former Yugoslavia, it's definitely for tourism. It would naturally be unfortunate if the industrious residents of these impoverished backwaters were to only participate in political tourism ventures as waiters and supporting actors.

I admit that there's also a personal dimension to my interest in the human imagination in times of crisis. I've been mulling over how to earn a dime too. I once met an unusual old woman who asked me a sly question.

"And where do you fit in: among the vampires or the donors?"

"I'm with the donors," I shot back in jest.

Today my off-the-cuff response turns out to have been the correct one. Because as the old woman explained it, people divide into two main groups: "vampires" and "donors." Being a donor doesn't automatically grant one the moral high ground, and neither does it relegate one to the loser category in advance. Maybe you're just lazy, and exposing your bulging veins to exploitation is easier than baring your teeth and getting down to work.

As someone with a donor's psychogram I've decided to try my hand as an entrepreneur. My idea is perhaps a little exclusive, but luckily for me it's not original. Originality, say marketing experts, only increases the risk of bankruptcy anyway. I've decided to rent out my soul. I'm well aware that the soul's value has fallen catastrophically, and that my business venture doesn't have much hope of success. But you never know. I'm inspired by the bright example of the Croatian businessman who with his dog food really has made a silk purse out of a sow's ear. My soul is flexible and displays strong regenerative properties. Its powers of absorption are as good as any old school blotter. Potential clients should provide a short biography. Perverts and smokers are out of the question. Payment in advance and in cash. Send contact details to the editor.

THE
CODE

YOU NEED TO know how to talk to small nations. At the recent Bosnian and Croatian premieres of her film *In the Land of Blood and Honey*, Angelina Jolie gave a master class in how it's done. As a film star Jolie could've done as she pleased, yet she acquitted herself with exceptional humility, declaring with complete sincerity that she'd fallen in love with Bosnia; that Bosnia had suffered terribly in a war started by the Serbs; yes of course, she added, the whole region had suffered too, in its own way. But she really got them when she said that she made the film (one not without cinematic merit) to showcase Bosnia's suffering to the world. Her words cooled the still gaping Bosnian wound like a balm.

She was a hit with everyone, the men in particular, so much so that no one noticed her deferential manner was the kind you put on when talking to children. With an unfailing human instinct, Angelina Jolie unlocked the code. She kissed the finger slammed in the drawer, gave the naughty drawer a good smack, *naughty, naughty drawer*, and the evil spirits slunk away. The Croats and Serbs waited in line with outstretched pinkie fingers, and I'm pretty sure that at least in their heads, the Slovenes, Macedonians, Albanians, and Montenegrins were all lining up somewhere too. Angelina Jolie blew them an air kiss. The Serbs were pissed and beat their fists in the dung heap: They'd expected more than just air.

If the rules of political correctness prevent us from abusing ethnic, national, racial, gender, and other types of differences—all unreliable in any case—and we're looking for something to fall back on, there's always *the code*. Social groups, tribes, sects, gangs, religious communities, mafia structures, families, Internet fan clubs, they're all characterized by codes of behavior—written and unwritten, conscious and unconscious, enduring and susceptible to change, respected and disrespected. If not by a code of social behavior, how might we explain why Americans—just for example now—almost never bellyache when meeting an acquaintance, but rather portray their lot in life as shiny and good, while Croats and other Yugozone[1] residents can't wait to start bitching the second they clap eyes on someone they know. If they're not whining about their personal problems—a toothache, a bad haircut, the long line at the post office that morning, a neighbor who turns his TV up too loud, a relative who landed in hospital, their kid who got an F at school— then they'll be bitching about rising prices. There's an authenticity to the bitterness there, because prices seem to go up every day. The thing is, however, the bitcher-in-question gives you the impression that the price rises are directed at him personally. His bitching and our attendant commiserations work like morphine on him. It's like

---

1 The Yugozone is my coinage for the region encompassing the disintegrated and disappeared former Yugoslavia. Someone recently came up with the term "Yugosphere," and although the meaning is the same, I still prefer Yugozone.

Yugozone residents spend their lives wandering around with a little finger outstretched, just waiting for someone to blow on it and give it a kiss. And when someone does, presto, the pain disappears as if it'd never been there.

Yugozone residents, the men in particular, all behave in a similar manner toward their leaders. The genius of Slobodan Milošević wasn't that he said *c'mon, let's go smash some Croats, Bosnians, and Albanians*, but that with an unfailing fatherly impulse he put his finger on the code and promised Serbs: *No one will dare beat you again*. The genius of Franjo Tuđman was not that he *created the Croatian state*, but the way he delicately positioned himself among the Croats, the very same way Milošević positioned himself among the Serbs. And Tuđman could even boast the advantage of a doctoral title. Yugozone residents love "doctors" and "generals" (*it's in our ganglions* is how my former countrymen like to put it, just because they like the word ganglions), because only "doctors" and "generals" can decree—sorry, I meant guarantee—that everything will be as it should. This explains a square in downtown Zagreb being called *Dr. Franjo Tuđman Square*, the doctoral honorific probably making the square a world first. Although a number of doctors and generals, beloved leaders of the Yugozone peoples, have met inglorious ends—one currently languishes in a jail in the Hague (Dr. Radovan Karadžić), another in a Zagreb jail (Dr. Ivo Sanader)—their political successors rely on the same code. Current Croatian President Dr. Ivo Josipović recently encouraged the almost half a million unemployed and disenfranchised Croats with the following: "Look after your health and fight for your rights." While this sort of tripe would sink anyone else on earth into a deep despair, Croatian workers took solace and comfort.

The consequences of behaving in accordance with the given code are as one might expect. Yugozone residents frequently elect *doctors* to represent them, and on a regular basis these *doctors* drag them into armed conflicts and other sundry financial and moral dead ends. And so the circle remains unbroken. It explains why in everyday life, for example, our "Yugozonian" will always stop the first passerby to ask for the street he's after. It wouldn't cross an American, German, or Englishman's mind—he's got his map, his guide, his iPhone. And I'm sure about all this, right? Absolutely! I myself am an exemplar of "transition," I've got my maps, guides, and iPhone, but I still prefer stopping the first passersby in the street. What's more, I get a vague sense of satisfaction in doing so, like I've outfoxed all the crap "other dumbasses" use.

Don't Yugozone residents, the men in particular, behave like children? For chrissakes, no way, that'd be an inadmissible colonial prejudice in our postcolonial time, a politically incorrect claim in these politically correct times. But the thing is, any observer, any Freudian amateur, might well hit upon the thought that Yugozone residents, particularly the men, are stuck in the cozy anal phase. What's more, it might occur to such an observer that Yugozone men don't want to grow up, which perhaps explains why they give their all to reduce those who have to their own height.

It was wise of Angelina Jolie to not linger longer in the Yugozone. Why? Because if she had hung around, the Yugozonians would've gnashed their teeth and bared their fangs. Naturally, they've got the softening-the-foreigner-up act down to a fine art. First of all you drown him in local wine (which is of course the best in the world), and then you stuff him with local food (also incidentally the best in the world). In the process you invent tribal customs (guests aren't allowed to refuse food or drink lest the host take offence), whistle local songs, pluck your *tamburica*, and wander around showing the alienated foreigner your region's natural beauty and miraculously weed-free local ruins. Finally you adopt and domesticate him: You turn Jeroen into Janko, John into Ivica, Angelina into Angie.

The Yugozonians will indulge in hearty backslaps with our foreigner, con him into partaking of imaginary local customs (we kiss five times here!), all until his muscles relent and soften, until he's pliable. And when they've finally reduced the foreigner to their own height, when they've got the foreigner well-marinated in their toxic slime (and Angelina's become Angie), it's only then that the symbolic mastication begins. Yugozonians hate everything foreign, they down only what's theirs, and if they do manage to get something new past their tonsils, then oh boy do they give it a mauling first. Albert Einstein, for example, to them he's just "our Bert," the guy who had a Serbian mother-in-law. That's the only way they can take him.

Yugozone residents, the men mainly, hate pretty much everything and everyone, yet stubbornly and irrationally insist that others love them. To the common sense question of why anyone might thus love them, and whatever happened to reciprocity in matters of the heart, oh don't worry, they're not lost for words, they've got a ready answer. They remember well those moments of unconditional love. They remember their mothers burbling—"Who did a big poo for Mummy? Who did a big poo for Mummy?" They remember their joyous kicking little feet and gurgling confession—"Gu-gu-gu-I-did-a-poo." The magnificence of this moment is forever fixed in their memory. And consequently, they delight in dumping every-where for as long as they might live.

THE DREAM
OF DORIAN GRAY

SHE SHOWS ME a photograph. In the photo are children from her class, the image taken at the end of the school year. She points to a sweet little face.

"Dora's the prettiest in the class," she says.

Dora's a little girl with long blond hair. My eight-year-old niece has short brown hair. She's staring at the photo, but she's all ears. I wonder what I should tell her. I know that responding with questions like "but is Dora smart?" or "is she a nice person?" won't help any in getting my message across. It won't help if I say, "no, I think you're the prettiest." There's some kind of consensus in her class that Dora is the prettiest and there's no disabusing her of this. The virus of insecurity has already wormed its way inside her.

"You're right, Dora's got pretty ears," I reply, though you can't see her ears in the photo.

Lookism is a widespread and devastatingly powerful prejudice based on a person's physical appearance. There have been attempts, unsuccessful of course, to have it placed in the same category as racism, classism, sexism, heterosexism, and ageism. It's a word with plenty of synonyms—aestheticism, physicalism, appearance discrimination—all signifying the same discriminatory practice: Fat people, short men, tall women, the elderly, the "ugly," are to be rounded up and herded into one of life's dark corners.

When I was my niece's age other little girls seemed more beautiful to me, too. Lidija had auburn hair and bushy eyebrows. Zlatica a light, translucent complexion, with tiny bluish veins below the surface. Jasminka full lips and oval baby teeth, shiny like silky candies. It was back then, in elementary school, that we all got it into our heads that the prettiest girl in the class was also the best little girl. With time the grind of everyday life bumped the painful subject of physical appearance from our list of priorities. The dream about the frog that turns into a princess, and those thousands of before-and-after photos that we absorbed like thirsty sponges, they worked in parallel, shunting our unconsciousness toward a hazy future in which we'd leave the miserable *before* far behind, and the desired *after* would last forever.

In the meanwhile, small women's sizes have become smaller, skinny women skinnier, cosmetic surgery more popular, and clothes for the fuller figure both harder to find and more expensive. If the Berlin Wall hadn't fallen, luxury Italian fashion designer Marina Rinaldi would've had to shut up shop. Today her clothes are all the rage with Europe's "Easterners," women whose husbands have made a quick mint in the intervening years. Rinaldi has boutiques all over Eastern Europe, even in Podgorica, the Montenegrin capital, where Russian women shop on their summer vacations, alongside the odd solvent, and more corpulent, Montenegrin woman. Weight is a class marker. Only poor people are fat. Fat is ugly because poverty is ugly. While the poor pack on the pounds, the wealthy remain elegantly hungry. Research suggests that every second American man would have no qualms about divorcing a fat wife. There's no mercy anywhere for the fat. Bloomingdale's in New York recently amalgamated their clothing section for plus-sized women with the one for baby clothing: Fat women are either pregnant, or losers who don't manage to wiggle into size Victoria Beckham the day they waddle out of the maternity ward. Saks Fifth Avenue is closing its plus size section Salon Z, formerly a temple of solace for the well-to-do fuller-figured woman. The message is clear: Being fat—right there next to being a smoker—is an intolerable social evil. Sometimes you see the fatal fusion on New York streets. The smoker will be the fat girl.

Let's be straight with one another now, ever since beauty stopped lying in the eye of the beholder and the marketplace began enforcing its own normative standards, the world has become a boring place. There are fewer and fewer unique faces around, all the interesting "honkers," "beaks," and other factory defects have pretty much disappeared. Gone are the men who stink of cigarettes, garlic, and sweat; hairy chests, beer bellies, and black vodka bags under the eyes have gone the same way. It's enough to cast a cursory glance over the gallery of new Russians making waves at home and abroad. Former KGB man, Alexander Lebedev, an oligarch who in 2010 bought the English *Independent* newspaper, is a well-read gentleman with stylish thin frame glasses on his nose. He looks more like an intellectual than an ex-spy. Punching a fellow guest on a Russian talk show and declaring that anyone who doesn't have a million dollars deserves to burn in hell hasn't harmed Lebedev's domestic or international reputation in the least. Alexander Mamut, a former

Yeltsin adviser who not so long ago bought the bookstore chain Waterstones, well he looks like a learned post-perestroika man of letters. Vladimir Doronin (Naomi Campbell's boyfriend), Roman Abramovich, even Mikhail Gorbachev, once the brains behind perestroika and today mascot for Louis Vuitton travel bags—these guys have all repositioned themselves. Not one of them looks how we might expect. Dorian Gray can rest easy; his dream has been realized. Even Mikhail Khodorkovsky, another Russian oligarch (albeit one who's languishing in jail for apparently no reason), has a pretty face adorned by thin frame glasses. He's become such an inspiration and icon of compassionate capitalism that celebrated Russian writer Lyudmila Ulitskaya has published a book of correspondences with this most capitalist of all martyrs, a fledgling saint. An Estonian composer has even composed a symphony dedicated to this most innocent of oligarchs. A Croatian taxi driver, a former *Gastarbeiter*, returned to his homeland, fiddled his way to an overnight million, managed to usurp public space for a private parking lot, killed three people (one with a car, two with a yacht), and yet still walks the streets a free man. He's svelte, has a permatan, and wears those smart glasses on his nose, too.

Today everyone is beautiful. Successful female tennis players are beautiful, and beautiful female tennis players successful; successful classical musicians are beautiful; violinists and cellists are beautiful; opera soloists give supermodels a run for their money; high-jumpers are beautiful; soccer players are sex symbols; Nadzeya Ostapchuk aside, even shot-putters have been going in for a makeover. Because aesthetic capital is critical for success. *Beauty Pays*—that's the unambiguous message of Daniel Hamermesh's book. Catherine Hakim, author of the bestselling *Honey Money: The Power of Erotic Capital*, argues the same. And research confirms it: Beautiful people earn more than ugly people, beautiful women are more likely to find a wealthy provider. Statistics suggest that our annual spending on cosmetics is enough to end global hunger, yet the question remains as to who's willing to give up their face cream for a noble cause. No one, I suspect. I wouldn't either. In any case, let the men first give up their weapons, much more is spent on them.

On the map of the body there are no zones outside the jurisdiction of aesthetic arbitrage. Enchanted by the charms of the surgeon's knife, and having modified their breasts, faces, eyelids, double chins, lips, jaw lines, stomachs, you name it, women now don't just want any old vagina, but a tight one, a neatly-mown one. There are plastic surgeons specializing in transforming everyday vaginas into pretty ones, tired old ones into rejuvenated, youthful ones. And with the standards of physical beauty clear and generally accepted by all, everyone can, if they want to, be beautiful. Boredom might yet prove the only resistance factor to this mass bodily beautification.

Maybe all this explains why women are presently so obsessed with their rears. New York women seem to love wearing teenager tights. A pretty ass in elastic, skintight leggings (let's forget for a second that they look like diving gear) gets way more attention than a pretty face. I spotted this kind of ass near Central Park and promptly joined a small throng who had stopped to let their admiring eyes glide along after her. Stylish in body-hugging tights and a snug leather jacket that barely made it to her waist, the ass's owner paraded Central Park like royalty. It was a Saturday, and the young woman was taking her dazzling erotic capital out for a walk.

A MIDDLE FINGER

I OFTEN GO shopping in Amsterdam's Osdorp district, mainly because I enjoy the long bike ride through the park on the way there. But the chance to head out on my bike isn't the only reason. I sit there in a café surrounded by drab residential buildings and shops, my gaze set on a sculpture of an ugly stone coil simulating a gush of water into a perennially dry fountain. There are countless Dutch housing estates built in the sixties like this one. Today they're home to immigrants and to elderly Dutch who in a distant time swallowed the line about prosperous, functioning social housing, and all the rest that goes with it. We eventually come to love our own poor choices, particularly if righting them requires too great an effort.

I sit there in a café with a depressing view, with a dishwater coffee, and waiters like you don't even get in Montenegro anymore. There's a lovely café with a calming view of the lake barely a hundred meters from here. Why then, do I slouch in this one? I do it for the three, four, or five specimens I encounter here; it depends on the anthropologist's luck. I imagine that I'm here on a secret research mission, that I'm on a periodic follow-up visit to confirm previous results. The men are all around my age, my "countrymen"—a word that makes me wince. Every morning they descend from their apartments in the surrounding tower blocks, landing here like paratroopers. My ear, a keen hunter for spoken nuance, remains bizarrely tone-deaf, unable to discern the region they're from. Maybe because they're too much *from there*, from some former Yugoslav backwoods. Their garishness and stubborn typologies eliminate linguistic or ethnic specificities; they're simply sons of the culture in which they grew into the men they are today.

Their clothes and gait give them away. Their faces are sponges that have soaked up the faces of the men they grew up alongside, one imprinted on the other. These faces bear the traces of fathers and grandfathers, maternal and paternal uncles, men from the neighborhood or village, from their army days, from their local bars, from their workplaces, the faces of their countrymen, friends, men you see in the newspaper, on the TV screen, the faces of politicians, generals, soldiers, murderers, criminals, thieves, the faces of all those who brought them here, to Amsterdam's Osdorp, where every day they descend from their apartments like paratroopers to drink their morning coffee among *their own*, because they don't have anyone else but *their own*. This is the ground they've been allocated, it's a rare occasion they make it downtown; they're not that keen in any case, curiosity's not their strong point. So they sit in their chairs, legs spread wide, faces radiating sovereignty over the territory conquered, bodies suggesting they've planted their flag. "Historically" settled, they liberate their hands from their pockets and gesticulate wildly. They rarely smile, but snigger often. A snigger is their defense, it's how they get one over each other, hide a momentary defeat; they're not capable of engaging in conversation of any length or depth, not even with their own, they've never learned. A snigger is a reprieve, an eraser with which they wipe clean what's been said, their own speech or that of another; a snigger turns everything into a josh. They frequently let out an *eee-he-hee, hee-eeh-hee*, spurring each other on, approving or condemning, a backslap and circle jerk. *Ehee-heee* . . .

They know everything, they've always known everything, no one needs to explain anything to them; they know it all *too well*. The first phrase out of their mouths is: *I've always said* . . . They talk about money, politics, sports. Sometimes they lose it a little, and sniggering as they go, exchange information about the horrors of health checks, prostate and rectal exams and the like. They rarely mention women, and if they do, it's to take the piss out of each other, like schoolboys. *Eee-he-hee, hee-eeh-heee*. They don't know what they're doing here, but they'll be going back, they've got a share in a house, an apartment, a bit of land somewhere, it'll be enough to survive on. The Dutchies will throw them a crumb or two, which by God they deserve, having blessed this country with their presence.

They drink coffee or slurp beer from the bottle, swap what they've read in the papers from down there, pick over the bones of Milošević, Tuđman, the present, Karadžić, Mladić, the future . . . When's *down there* getting into Europe? (*What the fuck do you care? You're already in Europe!*) They're the real victims of the war, and adding insult to injury they messed up their choice of country—they went from a small one to a smaller one, Christ, you can't even see the sun or moon from here. The Poles get ahead better than they do (*Goes without saying. Poles are like Jews*), even the Bulgarians are doing better (*Maybe so, but only the Bulgarian Turks, don't you know the Turkish mafia runs everything here?*), only Bulgarians would clean Dutch toilets, they wouldn't do it dead. They're the ones sucking the big one, sifting about here not knowing why, and *down there* everything's going for cheap, everything's been stolen or sold, foreigners have bought up the coast, and now they're schlinging their schlongs, raving and partying, polluting our ocean (*Whaddaya mean "ours" bro? Uh yeah, I meant the former "ours" . . .*). *Down there* foreigners are multiplying like Gypsies, that's what you get for not respecting your own—others start living it up . . . *Eee-hee, hee-eh-hee,* the whole world's gone crazy, and those fags have been breeding too, you don't know who's a man and who's a woman anymore (*You don't even know who's a Serb and who's a Croat! Look at that little shit on the Hema billboards . . . Who? You know who I mean, the little fucker's everywhere. That fag kid from Tuzla! Paić! Nah, it's Pajić, Nah bro, it's Pejić! If he was my kid I'd drown him with my own hands!*).

The trio of my countrymen wouldn't have heard of the "fag kid from Tuzla" if he hadn't been plastered all over sumptuous billboards for the Dutch chain *Hema*, advertising a push-up bra. But who is Andrej Pejić? Andrej Pejić was born in Bosnia the same year Yugoslavia fell apart and the war machismo and thievery began. Andrej Pejić, the child of a Serb mother and Croat father, immigrated to Australia, emerging from the slimy Balkan darkness as a new human species, as a brilliant unicorn, a divine lily, a god and goddess in a single body, a miraculous metamorphosis, an enchanting transgender beauty, the world's most famous catwalks falling at his feet. Pejić is a middle finger flipped at the land where he was born, a divine error to take one's breath away, a middle finger to Balkan men, and Balkan women, too. Pejić is a symbolic figure who at this very moment is tearing down cruel gender barriers faster and more effectively than all the gender activists, academics, and

advocates combined. Pejić is a middle finger to Catholicism, Ortho-
doxy, and Islam, a middle finger to myths of Balkan heroism, to
macho-martyrdom, a finger up the snouts of commanding officers,
police, thieves, and politicians. Andrej Pejić is a boy with breasts,
or a girl with a penis, or worse still: He's a Croatian woman with
a penis and a Serbian man with breasts, in a single body. Having
gotten as far away as one could ever get, Pejić has become a dazzling
ray of light for the tens of thousands of Yugoslav children dispersed
to the four corners of the world by the wars. I often run into them
on my travels: a smart girl from Pirot, hustling her way into an
academic career in Berlin, a lesbian; a finely-etched young man (the
son of a chest-beating, big rig-driving Serb and a cowering Croatian mother) conscientiously studying at Harvard, a homosexual; a
young guy from Banja Luka, a receptionist at the Hilton in London,
a Thai son-in-law and passionate reader of Hannah Arendt; and
many, many others . . .

My three from the café (just like their numerous male countrymen
down there) are still crapping on about politics, dribbling, gulping
their morning coffees or beers, sniggering away. Finally they get up,
thrust their hips out, linger over their goodbyes, let out an *eee-he-
hee, hee-eeh-hee*, just to carve their names into the indifferent surface
of the surrounding concrete, just to leave some kind of scrape to
mark their existence. Then they go their own ways, it's lunchtime.
They depart not understanding that they've been dead a long while
already, that the morning encounter with *their own* has been but a
brief outing from the grave.

WHO IS TIMMY MONSTER?

SOMEONE IN MY building in otherwise docile Amsterdam has been terrorizing the rest of us. How? Simply. Late at night and early in the morning the mystery man (or woman?) starts shunting furniture around his apartment. That's our best guess as to what's going on, we've got no way to be sure. There's just this ghastly scraping that penetrates every floor and apartment, its effect like an electric shock. We all think the racket's coming from the apartment directly above us. We suspect each other, and the more vociferous among us knock on doors, wag our fingers, and leave warning notes. We all plead innocence—no, it's not us. When the mystery man cranks up his racket, we vent our distress on the central heating pipes that connect all the apartments. The scraping falls silent for a second, as if it's received the message, and then the torture erupts again, more brazenly than before. We're at war. And what drives us most insane is that we don't know who our enemy is. For months we've been walking around with cupped ears, leaning against walls, none the wiser as to who's behind the damn scraping.

Yes, we're at war. Our fears multiply from one day to the next. They arrive as a scraping that makes the walls of our apartments quiver, they arrive via the television screen, the telephone, the Internet, Facebook, Twitter; the more we're wired together, the more our fears are fuelled, like gas balloons. We're all there on an invisible psychiatric couch.

I meet up with an acquaintance. She's approaching sixty, two adult sons. She and her husband are modest Dutch folk. For a time she worked as a teacher, and then she starting doing charitable work teaching young Moroccans Dutch. She does so firm in her belief that the cultivation of neighborly relations, a smile on the dial, and small interventions make life on planet earth a little more bearable. She was telling me about something new she'd been working on; touch therapy, something between tapping therapy and haptonomy. She does it with Moroccan kids, boys mostly, the kind who mark the territory out front of their tower blocks until late into the night, brawling and stealing, dishing out beatings and dreaming up child- ish ways of making others' lives hell. Sometimes it's defecating on a neighbor's doorstep, other times it's peeing up the door.

"What do you do with them?" I ask.

"I tap them a little, give them a hug, like a mother would her baby. Touch reduces aggression, you know that."

I look at my acquaintance—her face radiating a somewhat un- healthy enthusiasm—and I'm not sure what to make of it all.

There's definitely something not right with humanity. Some psy- chopath from Belgrade bought a little girl from her father for a thousand euro. Why? So he could rape her on a daily basis. In Texas a twelve-year-old strangled a four-year-old with a skipping

rope. Senior high school students from Karlovac raped a classmate
with a chair leg. A fifty-year-old from Zagreb garroted his seventy-
seven-year-old mother with a piece of wire. In a Croatian village a
grandson twice set fire to his grandfather's house, and eventually
pummeled him to death. A husband and wife with a three-year-
old jumped from the sixth floor of a Belgrade hotel. A French-
man bundled his three-year-old son into the washing machine and
turned it on. Why? The kid had been naughty.

Yes, there's definitely something not right with humanity. We each
haul an invisible psychiatric couch along with us. We seek understanding, yet few are ready to understand others. There's only the
market, ever ready to offer comfort. With every new year that rolls
around more and more people have started wishing each other
Happy New Fear. The words fear and stress have entered our everyday lexicon, like bread and milk. Fear of an itch, fear of the dark,
fear of noise, fear of madness, fear of pain, fear of open space, fear
of enclosed space, fear of the road, fear of crossing the road, fear of
sharp objects, fear of cats, fear of the opinions of others, fear of dust,
fear of driving, fear of insult, fear of looking up, fear of people, fear
of anger, fear of floods, fear of touch, fear of bees, fear of amputa-
tion, fear of numbers, fear of fire, fear of falling, fear of thunder, fear
of asymmetrical objects, fear of ruins, fear of failure, fear of filth,
fear of loneliness, fear of flying, fear of microbes, fear of steps, fear
of depth, fear of change, fear of mirrors, fear of bats, fear of money,
fear of food, fear of theft, fear of sleeping, fear of the grave, fear
of sweating, fear of glass, fear of animal fur, fear of crowds, fear of
knowledge, *epistemophobia*, fear of ideas, *ideophobia*, fear of speech,
laliophobia, fear of words, *logophobia*, fear of memories, *mnemophobia*,
fear of everything new, *neophobia*, fear of everything, *pantophobia* . . .

In a long ago episode of *The Muppets* the forgotten comic Zero
Mostel recites the Jerry Juhl-penned poem "Fears of Zero." Mostel
enumerates his manifold fears: fear of spiders, fear of dentists, fear
of baldness . . . Fear muppets appear from somewhere in the darkness and crawl all over Mostel, threatening to swallow him up.
Although terrified, Mostel insists that he needs to count his fears,
confront them, overcome them, and that they'll then disappear of
their own accord (*Once they are counted and compelled, they can quickly
be dispelled!*), and miraculously, they really do vanish. The fears were
figments of Mostel's imagination. Having dissipated his lesser fears,
Mostel senses that a new, greater fear is to come. And indeed one
does come along, in the form of Timmy Monster, and this time
Mostel's magic formula proves of no help. Mostel disappears and
from Timmy's stomach we hear his voice. Mostel admits that he's
just a figment of Timmy's imagination.

Humanity has never been more terrified than it is today. We each
haul our psychiatric couch along with us. People cry as if hit by tear
gas and withdraw into their safety zones. Computer screens are our
bunkers, the virtual world offering security, a place no one can reach
us. People hang out less and less frequently, they avoid relationships,
avoid touching, are scared of one another, intolerant of one another,
get along only with the greatest of difficulty. Of course some men
make appropriate arrangements and buy "real dolls," "boy toy dolls,"
"love dolls," perfect silicone partners. They sleep with their "babies,"
clothe them, bathe and comb them, take them out for walks, on
little adventures, spend the weekends with them, and occasionally take them in for repair. The wealthier are collectors and have
multiple partners. Some, like Kevin, are in complex relationships:
He keeps "real dolls" at home, and goes out with *organic* women.
Some claim the dolls are "perfect listeners," others that "they can't

get pregnant," others that a doll "improves quality of life," others are enchanted by their "beauty and stoicism," others maintain that only a doll is able to "love them in spite of everything." Gordon from Virginia dreams of joint burial ("We'll be turned into dust together, and it'll be a beautiful thing"). Matt, a doll maker, claims his handicraft is therapeutic, because it's better "to have sex with a piece of rubber than not have it at all."

Some women are also taking appropriate steps. The marketplace has provided them with "reborn dolls." At first glance it's hard to tell the difference between the artificial and the organic. Sharon Williams has a collection of forty-one such "babies," all one of a kind, totally unique, each sleeping in his or her own idiosyncratic way. Maybe these "baby" owners, these weirdoes and sickos, are the moral avant-garde of our time. Instead of shoving their children in the washing machine, or waiting for someone else to, it's possible these women have worked out that it's better they cradle and coddle hyper-realistic silicon surrogates. Perhaps the many aging mothers who have raced out to buy *reborn* babies are acutely conscious of the fact that they've given birth to potential monsters, who tomorrow might rape a classmate with a chair leg, so these women buy a comforting ersatz, a simulacrum. Reborn dolls, they say, "fill the emptiness in your soul," they don't scream, don't pee, don't let out a squeak, they don't grow up, they sleep an eternal sleep. Family life with them is straightforward, just sometimes you need to wipe the dust off them, position them, reposition them. Simulacra are simultaneously our defeat and our solace.

Manufacturers try their hands at making all kinds of stuff "life-like," from chocolate-scented USB sticks to strawberry-scented earrings. Autumn Publishing, for example, is preparing a collection of children's books, which they're going to call *Smellescence.* At the touch the books are to release the scents of chewing gum, berry fruits, and the like. "This advanced technology and the smells it creates are so real they take children's reading to a magical new level. We wanted to inject some fun into the reading experience and this is a powerful way to do just that," said company director, Perminder Mann. Given that farting has recently made inroads into children's publishing (*Walter the Farting Dog; The Gas We Pass: The Story of Farts; The Fart Book; Doctor Procto's Fart Powder,* and many, many others), Autumn Publishing is having a go with its own picture book, *The Story of the Famous Farter,* which on the last page is to smell like a lowdown, dirty ripper.

Yes, there's something not right with people. Whether with our voluntary acceptance of the virtual world we are to mutate into *different* people—just as pet kitties that play with artificial mice eventually turn into *different* kitties—it's hard to say. One thing is certain: We're all volunteers in a mega-experiment. We're all the figment of someone's imagination. And just as no one in my building knows who among us is making that hellish scraping, humanity doesn't actually know who the Timmy Monster is. Or it's pretending it doesn't know. What if Timmy Monster is all of us?

3.

ENDANGERED SPECIES

A dark and gloomy cesspool. And glowing in the cesspool are rotten stumps, phosphorescent mushrooms—fungi. These are our emotions! This is all that's left of our emotions, from the flourishing of our souls.

—*Yuri Olesha,* Envy

CAN A
BOOK SAVE
OUR LIFE?

ON A BRIEF visit to Jerusalem I walked the streets of Mea Shearim, one of the city's more colorful neighborhoods, home to the Haredi Jews. The ingenuous tourist could be forgiven for thinking that he or she has strayed onto a film set depicting the life of a nineteenth-century Jewish shtetl. But life in Mea Shearim is for real, preserved the way it was a hundred years ago. Those who live in the neighborhood don't try to cash in on their exoticism; tourists are (for now) unwanted. My eye caught a trio of skinny, pallid-looking men in tall black hats, all draped in black frock coats. They stood there in a circle as if mumbling the words of a prayer in unison. One cradled a weighty leather-bound tome. As he opened the Torah (and I'm guessing here), I noticed that the book was actually a hollowed-out cavity, a box camouflaged inside a book. Inside the book wrist watches shimmered. This little detail cheered me no end, and for a moment I thought I had turned up in the Odessa of Isaak Babel's stories.

In May 2011, the Argentine artist Marta Minujín exhibited her installation *Torre de Babel de Libros* on San Martín Square in Buenos Aires. Fashioned from books from all over the world, the tower was twenty-five meters high. Croatian newspapers proudly published a list of all the Croatian titles in the project, as if the whole thing was about the massive international success of Croatian literature. Yet the mytheme of the Tower of Babel points to the opposite: failure. Nimrod, a descendant of Noah, initiated the building of the tower out of a desire to create "a city and a tower, whose top may reach unto heaven." Enraged by the hubris and unbridled ambition of it all, Yahweh destroyed the tower and punished its builders by giving them different languages, short-circuiting access to Google Translate along the way. The story goes something like that, perhaps a little different.

One way or another, books have always been multifunctional: Depending on the user they have been good for kindling, bonfire fuel, brownbagging, bookshelf supports, wine coasters, secret piggy banks, status symbols, and/or window cleaning paper. Marta Minujín is far from alone—many contemporary visual artists have used, abused, and defamiliarized books in different ways. In one of Richard Wentworth's cerebral installations, books hang by string from the ceiling, in others, broken plates, hand watches, and candy wrappings jut out like strange bookmarks. Jonathan Safran Foer's latest book, *Tree of Codes*, is an artistic installation affordable to all. Foer has disemboweled every page of his favorite bedside reading— Bruno Schulz's *The Street of Crocodiles*—creating a "window" on each page that alters the meaning of the original text. Having suffered this "vandalistic" artistic treatment, Schulz's book has ended up a new, original work, one authored by a "vandal," just like Duchamp's moustachioed Mona Lisa.

Video clips currently making the rounds of the Internet also make keen use of "vandalistic" narration. In *Can a Book Save Your Life* a professional shooter fires a revolver into a handful of recent books, testing how *bulletproof* they are. Another, *Bill Simmons' Book Can Save Your Life!*, proves that, shot with a 9 mm revolver, Bill Simmons's book really can. The Spanish clip *Did You Know the Book?* takes up the apparent end of the Gutenberg era, a likeable young sales rep presenting the book as a completely new product and explaining its advantages—no wires, no batteries, no viruses, easy to read, easy to handle. There is a Norwegian clip with a similar message. In a monastery library somewhere, an older monk is having trouble getting to grips with a book, bringing to mind the struggle early adopters endured with the computer. A younger monk patiently explains to the elder how one uses it, but then loses his cool and leaves him an instruction manual. These examples—some of which have been randomly selected from the cultural mainstream, and others equally randomly from its fringes—clearly point to both the death of the book and the death of literature itself (the latter having died the moment it turned into—"books," i.e., merchandise). Yet authors (better known in the publishing world as content providers), book industry employees (who used to be called publishers), and consumers (until recently referred to as readers) aren't exactly going quietly into the night—a desperate resuscitation of the corpse is underway, a final shakedown for the last penny.

The more irremediable the death of the book becomes, the more wild and flailing the resuscitation effort. The publishing industry is producing a greater number of books, and is doing so faster than ever before. The good old days when literary bestsellers appeared every few years, or maybe once a year, are irrevocably past. Today global bestsellers burn brightly on a monthly basis, and then fizzle as fast as New Year's firecrackers. Overnight fame and hefty advances reserved for the few lucky puppies are no longer a secret, and neither are the annual earnings of the industry's top producers.[1] All this whets the appetites of the millions of hungry rookies. The examples of jackpot debutants suggest that anyone can make it if they want to, one just needs a little bit between the ears, good looks, a little luck—and spectacular (and spectacularly speedy) canonization is guaranteed.

The production of books has increased to the point that books are rarely actually read, let alone seriously evaluated. Anonymous commentators on Amazon.com (a few brief comments, *like it—don't like it*, little stars), bloggers, twitterers (even briefer comments), and even authors themselves have taken over critical duties. In the *Guardian* series of clips *Review My Book!* authors gush about why it is that *their* book should be reviewed, the end result being the desired (self-)review. It isn't easy for writers to reconcile themselves with their disappearance from the literary scene, their drowning in an endless ocean of other authors and books. Many are taking matters into their own hands. Some go in for self-promoting videos, or, if you're Umberto Eco, you revise an old book and create a digested and simplified Kindle-friendly edition (*The Name of the Rose*)—self-resuscitation at its most panicked. In fear of evanescence, many dream up wacky passions or hobbies, this kind of supplementary authorial trace is a way to expand the club of devotees and potential readers. Some come out swinging for the protection of panda bears,

---

1   According to Forbes magazine, in 2010 James Patterson took top honours with $84 million in earnings, followed by Danielle Steel ($35 million), Stephen King ($28 million), Janet Evanovich ($22 million), and Stephenie Meyer ($21 million), with young adult novelists Rick Riordan, Jeff Kinney, and Suzanne Collins further down the list.

others vegetarianism, others worry about global warming—and some will do whatever it takes. In a television interview Charlotte Roche—the best-selling author of (in her own phrase) "the hemorrhoid novel" *Wetlands*—popped her partial denture out, showing viewers her missing front tooth, tossed the denture high in the air, caught it in her mouth, and settled it back in place with her tongue. The audience went into rapture.

This world wouldn't be hurtling along with such speed were its own destruction not constantly at its heels—this is the sentiment of the anonymous collectively authored manifesto *The Coming Insurrection*. The literary world is no longer a space of contemplation, subversion, spiritually enriching escapism, or discovery, but one of spectacle. Nor is the book any longer "the temple of the soul"—it is a bare-assed commodity little different from a bottle of Coca-Cola. Writers can be ticket holders in the lottery, daydreamers, clued-up entrepreneurs, intellectual proles, exhibitionists, content providers, whatever, but like it or not, they are all participants in the society of spectacle. Measured by its yardsticks, they divide into winners and losers.

On the subject of Coca-Cola, there's a good joke from the repertoire of Cold War humor. Ronald Reagan is woken in the middle of the night:

"Mr. Reagan, sir, the guys from the evil empire are up painting the moon red!"

"What the hell?!"

"The Russians are on the moon and they're painting it red!"

"Get our boys up there and write 'Coca-Cola' on it, pronto," Reagan replies groggily.

If we leave the political connotations of the joke to the side (these days even the gung-ho Chinese are into graffiti!), then the mytheme of the Tower of Babel appears ghostly on its semantic field. The world is divided into losers—who clamber toward the moon seduced by the poetic idea of painting it red—and winners just waiting to write Coca-Cola on a red backdrop. Losers win the right to the consolation of "symbolic capital," the winners get the fame and money. Until recently the realization of "symbolic capital" underpinned the entire literary system, with its evaluatory codes, publishers, critics, theorists, translators, university literature departments, journals, literary prizes and so forth. Today that system is in ruins. Hope is gone; getting paid is all that remains. And as far as the book goes, yes, a book can save your life. But only if it is *bulletproof.*

A WOMEN'S CANON?

NOT SO LONG ago I found myself in Norway at the invitation of the Norwegian association of literary critics. The Norwegian critics were all in a lather, the old-fashioned word *canon* buzzing in the air. My hosts were embroiled in voting to select a Norwegian canon, ten works representative of Norwegian national literature. The results were disheartening: Eight of the writers were men, only two were women. I had very short odds on the Norwegians being far more progressive on the gender question, which I guess explains my disappointment.

National literatures are—irrespective of (or perhaps as a result of?) globalization—in fighting form. National canons are organized like soccer teams. The players are men. And the referees are too. The winners of the ever-swelling number of literary prizes are inevitably men. But now they make sure prize juries have a more-or-less equal number of men and women, so when a man again lifts the trophy, no can say it was a gender fix. The European literary canon is in fine fettle. Its representatives are men, too.

They say that literature is a hobby right up until the author's literary message reaches its recipient. But to whom do we send our artistic messages? Women writers most often cite men as their literary idols. Men almost never cite women as theirs. Research confirms that men never, or only very rarely, read books by women. Having carefully collated the data, VIDA, an American women's literary organization that crunches the numbers on gender discrimination in literature, concluded that three-quarters of books reviewed in prestigious American newspapers and magazines were written by—men. Women's Studies is no longer an academic eccentricity as it once was, but rather an academic necessity. Feminism and postcolonialism instigated the long process that eventually led to an increased awareness of the gendered and racially colonized nature of women's cultural history. Today, young women writers from Africa, South America, and Asia, their print runs the envy of literature's canonized men, raise their flags from all corners of the contemporary cultural map. And moreover, their gender, ethnic, and religious identities— serious hindrances until recently—today serve to enhance their commercial clout. A woman is awarded the Nobel Prize for Literature about once every ten years.

But have women managed to establish their own "cultural canon," or something that might be called "women's culture"? How do women perceive themselves today? Which prominent women do they mass identify with? Who are their female cultural icons? What causes do they advance, for what are they pushing, and who are they addressing? While we're at it, to whom am I sending my literary messages?

Be they women or men, who are my potential readers? How do they see me?

In contemporary culture women still construct their cultural values on self-colonizing assumptions. Let's run through a few female icons, who in our "in today, out tomorrow" world are, of course, easily substituted. Hugging the beloved American *before* and *after* formula, Oprah Winfrey went from being a dumpy, promiscuous, sexually-abused, and deprived young woman to a slim and sexy mistress of the small screen, one of the most influential women in America. Diana, "the Princess of Hearts," now a somewhat faded icon, crippled by the brutal rituals of royal everyday life, ended hers in a tragic traffic accident. Hillary Clinton, today a sun that is setting, maintained her dignity throughout the scandal of her husband's infidelity, held her family together, and emboldened, went on to win new political victories. Paris Hilton (not to mention the plethora of lookalikes!), a *celeb* who resembles a cheap statuette of the Virgin Mary sold at a newly-built church, she's "a victim of the media," a symbol of emptiness, one whose every move is followed by every tabloid in the world. Frida Kahlo (and a long line of contemporary female artists boasting the same "aura") is a "martyr" whom the culture industry has transformed into a "saint."

The self-victimization (and here we need to bear in mind that "victimization" is a broad term, one some cultural theorists also claim includes shopping) formula women use to win green cards for entry into the orbit of cultural icons is worryingly patriarchal. A fleeting glance at many female public personalities (pop-stars, actresses, models, artists) reveals that beneath the star's shine—in a camouflaged, perverted, or real shape—crouches the figure of the female "martyr." Even a third-grade pop-starlet knows the drill: Slip a sextape to the media, accuse the same media of destroying her moral integrity, then kick back and watch her popularity skyrocket. Why? Because of a homemade sextape? No—because she's done the perp walk of public humiliation and emerged from the other side, into the glow of moral redemption. Mainstream women's culture presently revolves around traditional dialectic formulas of whore–virgin–martyr–saint, the stuff of men's wet dreams, dreams served up to them by women.

Think of the manifold TV series, films, books, and celebrities, that owe their status as walking cultural texts to the media. Like a virus, the same formula also lies hibernating in so-called "serious" literature, from classic novels by men (*Anna Karenina, Madame Bovary*) to romance novels, which are chiefly written by women for women. The same formula might also explain why women dominate the memoir genre, and why it is mostly women who read them. As a genre, the memoir is built on the very same religious-confessional basis.

Women "colonize" themselves, adapting themselves to the stereotype of woman-as-victim (or are they authentically such?), because it seems that communication with the world only works when packaged as such. With the likes of Frida Kahlo as their icon, time and time again women double down on their symbolic capital, the martyr Kahlo having replaced Sylvia Plath (who in the 1970s united the feminist world like a magnet) in the millennial turn. Kahlo's "Diego on My Mind," a self-portrait in which Kahlo bears a miniportrait of Diego Rivera on her forehead, proffers an unsettlingly powerful message about a woman in whose life the central role has been given over to a man. But Sylvia Plath might have painted a similar picture, a portrait of Ted Hughes on her forehead. Taking home a literary prize, a Croatian woman recently told reporters: "I hope I didn't win the prize because I'm a woman." "I hope I didn't win the prize because I'm a man" is a sentence uttered by—no man ever!

Female role models in the cultural field are rarely emancipatory, they just pretend to be. In truth, whether a particular model has an emancipatory effect or not is largely dependent on the media, political, and cultural context. I look back with nostalgia at Erica Jong's *Fear of Flying*, which, at least for my generation, had an emancipatory effect. Some thirty years later, Eve Ensler's *The Vagina Monologues* boasted the same emancipatory force. Yet my cultural experience read the latter (particularly the edition in which Ensler included readers' responses, such as the ecstatic "I'm my vagina! My vagina that's me!") as retrograde. *Fear of Flying* emerged at the time of the sexual revolution, its effect liberating. *The Vagina Monologues* emerged when social mores had already changed—when talking publicly about one's vagina was all the rage, and lighting a cigarette in a public place a criminal act.

In the meantime, the market has nurtured new niches such as chick lit, a mutant somewhere between Erica Jong and the traditional romance novel, one aimed at younger women. Both as readers and writers, women have shown themselves more open to new literary worlds, perhaps because they haven't had to worry about their place in national literary canons. They've never had seats at that particular table, so they're not angling for one. Many genres, which even thirty years ago were not deigned worthy of attention, have today become part of the literary and academic mainstream. It seems many of these "subliterary genres" (itself a vanished term!) have had a greater emancipatory function than middle-class culture, the consumers of which dutifully buy the annual Booker winner, stock up on something by the Nobel laureate, watch Oscar-winning movies, and try and catch whatever's hot at MoMA or the Tate Modern. But in a Barbie culture, Lara Croft appears to offer many young women greater emancipatory pleasures.

While there may be no such thing as a women's literary canon, there are certainly "women's classics," today given second lives in film and TV adaptions, and in new editions that could well serve as a solid fundament for a women's literary canon. Virginia Woolf and Jane Austen would be joined by shooting literary stars such as Zadie Smith, who, as industry and critical darlings, have seen their work promptly affirmed as contemporary classics. In this sense, canonization of women writers is already occuring, and with greater speed and ease than ever, but what does this mean in terms of a women's canon? In order to survive in the market, every culture is required to have a "negotiable" and "inclusive" character. If "women's culture" appears discontinuous (the tape rewound every ten years), might this perhaps be ascribed to the non-existence of a canon? But who might nurse such a canon into existence? The nation? The academy? Men? The market? And whose canon would it be anyway? A white women's canon? And how does one even approach the subject of a canon when the fundamental question of women's identity remains obscured. A woman's identity is inseparable from questions of class; for the age of patriarchy, one that is unhealthily obstinate and enduring, this is what it is constructed on—not gender.

Seismic political changes such as the fall of the Berlin Wall, the end of communism, or the disintegration of the former Yugoslavia, have adversely affected women, turning their lives upside down. The differences between me, who came of age in socialist Yugoslavia, and my young fellow countrywomen (be they Croatian, Serbian, Bosnian, or other) are today immeasurably greater than between me and West European or North American women of my age. My culture was a culture of books, the culture of my young female compatriots is that of the screen and the Internet; I was and remain an atheist, which is the most natural thing in the world to me; today they undergo religious induction (be it Catholic, Orthodox, or Muslim), as if this were the most natural thing in the world; I grew up in the conviction that the right to abortion was the most natural thing in the world, they grow up confronted by church-fuelled doubts and public debate on annulling this right; I grew up in the conviction that prostitution was unacceptable, they grow up listening to proponents of its legalization; I grew up in the conviction that the question of ethnic identity was irrelevant; they learn that it is one of prime importance; I grew up in the conviction that men and women were equal; they, I sense, grow up in the conviction that men and women have different roles, and that they need to work this to their advantage.

To whom, therefore, do I send my "messages"? Who are my potential readers, be they male or female? I live in a "nowhere" zone. It is from this nowhere zone that I send out my "messages in a bottle." My books have been translated into a number of foreign languages, a significant bonus for the literary critic lying dormant inside me. On the basis of my own example I'm able to track a book's fate, how it communicates with different linguistic and cultural milieux, how the same things are read in different ways in different milieux and at different times. I'm able to observe how atrophy or the absence of reception in one milieu doesn't necessarily mean a book's death, but rather the opposite, its right to a new life and reception in another. On the basis of my own work I'm able confirm the truth of Bulgakov's poetic thesis that "manuscripts don't burn": Texts might indeed "age" in one readership community, yet be invigorated when thrown into another. Being anchored in this nowhere zone, the absence of a target readership constituted by age, gender, ethnic, or religious identity, and translation into foreign languages have enabled me to observe the ways in which cultural texts speak and negotiate with each other, how they are read by each other, how they are imprinted in a different culture, the exchange that takes place, their circulatory routes, how they are revitalized, how they cut across the soft borders of all identities, and how in the end, together with many other books, they are gradually incorporated into the foundations of a future literary house that might someday be called transnational literature.

What am I talking about? Isn't my cultural enthusiasm somewhat exaggerated? Aren't things actually at a standstill, and it just seems to me that they're moving ahead? Because women—delighted anew every time by the fact that they've been given the cultural floor— forget to ask themselves what routine they are performing and, if the audience is applauding, why they are applauding.

The "Simplon Express Zagreb–Paris" was one of several artistic projects Croatia presented to the French public in the autumn of 2012, with Croatian artists journeying by train between the two capitals. A newspaper article on the event piqued my interest,

particularly a section about the performance of a young Zagreb artist, who masturbated in the train, "completely imperceptibly, sitting
with legs crossed and tensing her abdominal muscles."

"The education system doesn't teach us about sexuality, but we're
surrounded by pornography on every corner. Women have always
been objects of observation, a fact further reinforced by the expan-
sion of film, pornography inevitably being made exclusively by men.
The problem is that no one ever considers a woman's pleasure. I
self-pleasured in the train because a train really is an exciting means
of travel, and the invisibility of the act made me feel very powerful,"
the young artist explained her artistic concept to reporters.

The artist is convinced that her artistic project is both feministi-
cally and artistically provocative, even though (or perhaps because)
it is—"invisible." For those with slightly longer cultural memories
and experience, hers is simply a dull recycling project. Over the
past fifty years female artists have staged similar performances
in many places, Croatian artists among them. The artist's project
reveals not only her naivety, arrogance, and unwillingness to bone
up on her predecessors, but also an absence of context and continuity, the absence of will to build continuity. The episode speaks
to a humiliating artistic and intellectual apathy. And in this sense,
it is indeed a very "female narrative." Because without a women's
canon (now why wouldn't that be a word for continuity?), ambitious
and lazy little girls will go around in circles repeating the same
thing over, determinedly claiming that they're doing something
new. The absence of a canon, that is, the presence of discontinuity,
leaves an empty space that enables the inevitable reinscription of the
female, the production of an exhausted art that resorts to the same

stammering vocabulary, self-convinced that it is declaring revolution. In any case, a canon exists to be destroyed—and so that there is an awareness of what is being destroyed.

Stereotypes about women and women's creativity, even those (ostensibly) emancipatory, are ardently encouraged by men. Almost every male writer or critic will benignantly support "literary trash" written by women, his agenda two-fold: the first, promulgation of the myth that women are best at writing literary "trash" (which concomitantly serves to secure his own manly place on the shelves of "serious literature"), the second, to demonstrate that he, personally, has nothing against mass culture, which for him is code for women's equal participation in literature. Our literary man will cite Hannah Arendt at least once in his life, because she is the only woman he deigns worthy of citation. At least once in his life our literary man will serve on a jury, and in the process fight tooth and nail to ensure a woman doesn't win, and if she really must, then he'll do all in his power to ensure that the woman who does win will be she who least deserves it. Having done so, our literary man has then done his duty: Women have participated in literary life.

Stereotypes about women are most often promulgated by women themselves, because doing so is the surest path to money and attention in any field, literature included. Having attained a social standing from which they could effect change, declared feminists most often carry on like bordello owners, feeding men's fantasies and satisfying men's desires. Any number of women are employed in prominent positions in the Croatian media, yet this hasn't changed its content or appearance in any significant respect. In fact, the Croatian media is more pornographic and more corrupt than ever before—it's spent the last two decades trying to turn ninety-two-year-old Žuži Jelinek into a national women's icon. (Every nation needs its own Dr. Ruth!) Now who is Žuži? Žuži is a seamstress who hustled her way to becoming the milliner of choice for the Yugoslav women's communist elite, she's the author of *Secrets of a Well-Dressed Woman*, the first book of its kind in post-WWII Yugoslavia, she's a successful widow who has married four times, and she's a columnist with a specialty line in instructive feuilletons on women's life. Žuži's retrograde, semi-pornographic and semi-literate columns have made her a darling of the new Croatian media establishment. Often called upon as a public speaker, a year or so ago, at the invitation of a female law professor at the University of Zagreb, Žuži gave a lecture to female students—future lawyers—on her favorite topic: how the ideal woman should behave in marriage (unmarried women, naturally, don't fit into the "ideal" category). Above all, ideal women must satisfy their husbands' desires, meaning they have to be—dolls. On the subject of dolls, fifteen-year-old Venus Palermo, a little Lolita and embodiment of the teenage "living doll" craze, uploaded her own doll make-up instructional video to YouTube. Some thirty million visitors have now watched how they might turn themselves into dolls. "It makes me happy that I can inspire so many people," said Venus. This kind of woman, irrespective of whether a little girl or little old lady, is usually given media time in order that they might inspire other women. This time is frequently given to them by other women, "female pimps."

Nonetheless, every now and then women wake from their slumber, take a look around, and ask themselves what kind of world they're living in. In a recent article American writer Meg Wolitzer pointedly raised the culture's neglect of women writers relative to their male colleagues.[1] Although we can readily agree with her every observation, we remain struck by the fact that, in terms of her literary references, Wolitzer thinks of literature as an exclusively Anglo-American domain. It's as if she's forgotten the power relations involved; that the names of "neglected" American women writers appear in the window displays of every bookstore on earth; that it's probably all the same to a Korean woman writer whether she is discriminated against by her male colleagues at home, their Anglo-American buddies, or Anglo-American women writers.

Whatever the case may be, having first "satisfied men's desires," women eventually start asking the questions their predecessors asked long ago, to which—who would have thought—they never got any answers. And while women are preoccupied asking questions, men amuse themselves with the toys they have usurped, claiming that they're playing for all of us, that their game has universal significance. Like soccer, literature is their game. Why? Because they give themselves the right, because the right is given to them. By whom? By women, naturally.

---

1   Meg Wolitzer, "The Second Shelf," *The New York Times*, March 30 2012.

ZAGREB
ZOO

LATELY ALL THE talk has been about the decline of independent book-shops, the fall of the once powerful chains, publishers going to the wall, editors losing their jobs, the closing of libraries and university literature departments, literature PhDs on food stamps—but most of all, talk has been about the physical disappearance of books. Spokespeople for the two main views are plentiful: On the one hand, "the pessimists" furiously attack the aggressive "trash" pol-luting our cultural habitat and depriving it of oxygen, and on the other, "the optimists" furiously defend the laws of the literary mar-ketplace (the lowest category of optimist having recently tried to put *The Muppets* film in the dock for indoctrinating American children with anti-capitalist propaganda). People are all abuzz about tablets of all kinds, about self-publishing, the hordes of "non-professional" writers on the literary scene, among them the writers of fan fiction, which, as a *Guardian* headline beams, promises to be a "rich vein for publishers," one that suggests publishers are vampires ever on the lookout for fresh blood.

Amid the general clamor no one, really no one, is talking about writers, which means that the "workers" (the literary proletariat) have become a totally marginal factor in the chain of production. The proletariat has in any case disappeared from general view, both actual and mental, and can today only be seen in industrial museums; a wax figure clasping a symbolic hammer, a placard saying he's a worker, a man in a yellow helmet, wheeled out from the murk of forgetting for Labor Day celebrations. As far as the literary proletariat goes, let's recall the old Robert Altman film, *The Player*, in which an unscrupulous Hollywood mogul murders a screenwriter with impunity, marries his girlfriend, and then cynically claims that, in the film business, writers just get in the way. What was once a satire on a possible reality has today become reality. I cried watching my murdered colleague David Kahane draw his last breath in a parking lot.

Lately I've been meeting my fellow writers in unexpected places of work. On a recent trip to New York, three writers told me how they keep a roof over their heads with parallel careers as physiotherapists and masseurs. In Europe, there are a bunch of writers driving taxis. For example, a while ago an Irish taxi driver picked me up from Galway Airport and recited a long poem in praise of Irish-American relations. Fine, that's the Irish for you, I thought to myself, they're all born poets. However, in London, a taxi driver recently gave me a detailed rundown on half his novel. Hurrying to a literary evening in Brussels, I took a taxi only to find a professional writer sitting at the wheel, a Portuguese, driving to somehow make ends meet. And these guys weren't just wannabe writers like, for example, the Pakistani in Edinburgh who told me about how his girlfriend had left him, and then presented me with three possible synopses of the event. "I hate memoirs, I'd rather turn my memories into a script for a Bollywood film," he said, while driving me to the airport.

Historically speaking, writers have always fallen into the category of "sensitive" human material, but somehow they've hung on, surviving hostile epochs, the reigns of kings, czars, and dictators, seasons of book burnings and censorship. Today, lo and behold, some earn fabulous money and turn up on the *Forbes'* list of richest "content providers," tour the world like royalty, surrounded by clubs of devoted subjects. Ever since a few writers made it into star-like orbit, the writerly profession has become somewhat chic. Once upon a time only the shady took up the pen; the mad, potential suicides, masochists, and unemployed aristocrats in need of something to fill the day. Today money and fame have made writing an attractive occupation. To be like J. K. Rowling is equally if not more attractive than being like Angelina Jolie. You know, literature still has a few shares in our collective spiritual capital. Some great writers have posthumously become an integral part of the tourist package, Joyce in Dublin, Proust in Paris, for example. As a consequence of this apparent promise, many writers patiently endure semi-anonymity and poverty, their hopes firmly planted on life after death—their very own statue for local pigeons to crap on.

All in all, the fact is that today roses only bloom for the few. As a specific human species, the majority of writers are facing extinction. Whether writers fall into the *critically endangered* group like Sumatran orangutans; the *endangered* group like Malaysian tigers; the *vulnerable* group like African elephants; the *near threatened* group together with the jaguar; or in the *least concern* group with the giraffe—let's leave that to the experts. They say that the endangeredness of a species is determined by three factors: habitat, over-exploitation, and other risk factors such as threat of viruses. Every *former* literary theorist, critic, or historian (the *active* are as endangered as writers) will easily identify the same three threat factors at work in the literary world.

I see my writerly colleagues struggling more and more: some to hold on to their critical and popular status, others to win such status. Isabel Losada spent a few days in the window of a Paris bookstore promoting her latest book. She called the stunt *writer-in-residence*. Many writers take writer-in-residence jobs on tourist cruises, in hospitals, at universities and on safaris. I know of one author who has recently passed her safari guide test, and is now successfully combining two jobs, the literary and the touristic. A recent ad for a writer-in-residence program in prisons drew well over a thousand applicants. You get a two-year contract, and have to give creative writing workshops to prisoners two-and-a-half days a week. I personally know a writer who spent a year in a village famous only for its prison. The local authorities set her up with a pretty cottage and modest monthly stipend. In return, she was expected to write a book about her experience in the village.

Only some thirty years ago West European writers routinely mocked socialist realism as a genre and the Stalinist practice of placing Soviet writers in a factory, on a *kolkhoz*, or at a site where a motorway or dam was being built. Today these same West European writers dream of commissions from the likes of Shell or Heathrow. The most lucrative commissions circulating among a select group of Dutch writers come from the directors of big companies and banks (who might want to flavor an important meeting with a few words of wisdom, a poem or the like, and thus seek out "professional" help). Dutch writers dream of jobs as editors-in-chief at Shell or Heineken's in-house newsletter. Of course, today they don't call it a Stalinist socialist realist practice, but a successful business arrangement. No one has a moral crack at the lucky colleague; they envy him. What's more, in Amsterdam there's a literary agency that specializes in these kinds of literary gigs. Russian writers had the metal to mock Stalinist cultural practice, and did so masterfully (Ilf and Petrov, Mikhail Zoshchenko, and others). It's interesting that today few writers raise their voices against anything.

I've been carefully following the phenomenon of transition for the past twenty years or so, the transformation of a former communist country into a capitalist statelet. That statelet is called Croatia. Aside from the unemployed and those on a pension, the rest of the population consists of children, an extensive bureaucracy, a plethora of politicians, and a handful of local tycoons. The short story is that for the majority of the population things have gone downhill over the past twenty years, and only improved for a statistically negligible minority. On the other hand though, in the same period, the status of animals at Zagreb Zoo has improved markedly. While public services have been asset-stripped and closed down (a handful of Croats enriching themselves in the process), only the fortunes of animals at the Zagreb Zoo have been on the up. How is that? Simple: Wealthy Croats have taken protection of individual animals upon themselves. The owner of a well-reputed Zagreb restaurant has been feeding the tiger; the President the ostrich; a famous pop-starlet the flamingo; the tapir is under the protection of a well-known war criminal, while the crocodile is under the wing of a Croatian tycoon. Wealthy Croats amuse themselves to no end with conversations such as: *How's your ostrich? Good thanks, last month we nursed his sore throat back to health. And how's your tapir? I gave him up, now I'm looking after a hippopotamus. That basketball player took the tapir on . . . somehow suits him better.*

In citing the example of Zagreb Zoo, I naturally don't want to suggest that endangered writers should be put in zoos. But I don't see the problem with luxury resorts, theme parks, and writers' villages. I mean, in Soviet times there was such a village, romantic wooden cottages and the like. It was called Peredelkino. There, thirty years ago, in Boris Pasternak's former dacha I met the woman who served as the inspiration for the character of Lara in *Doctor Zhivago*.

While we're on the subject of Russians, let's put it out there that the Russians have always had more respect for literature than other nations. When you tally things up, no one, out of fear of the literary word—that is, respect for the literary word—has killed more writers than the Russians. That's why it's somehow understandable that a Russian oligarch has bought Waterstones, another the *Independent*, and a third set up a foundation for the translation of Russian writers into foreign languages (the same guy who one night paid Amy Winehouse a million pounds to sing just for him). Inspired by these examples, perhaps Madonna might swoop down to offer lifelong protection to a potential African Nobel laureate, or Bill Gates spend the rest of his days dedicated to the promotion of Malaysian literature.

So it's not all glum, you just need a little imagination. I really don't know why I'm so worried about writers. Being a writer is still predominantly a job for the boys. The assumption that things will be better for me if I'm my male colleagues' keeper is wrong: For them, my male colleagues, things will always be better. So why am I worrying, then? In an ocean of general despair, it's like worrying about the last European leper colony on the Romanian side of the Danube. I don't know, it must because I'm doing okay. I just passed my taxi driver training.

WHAT IS AN AUTHOR MADE OF?

WRITER AND/OR AUTHOR?

Look at the years I've clocked in—and I'm still not sure about the name of my profession, or even what it's for! If earnings qualify a particular human activity as a profession, then only a small number of writers can claim writing as theirs. Yet even so, the true purpose of the profession remains painfully unclear. Perhaps this uncertainty of purpose can be traced to the literary creator's schizophrenic split into author and writer. In the 1970s, Roland Barthes's "The Death of the Author" upended literary scholarship and even today the text remains one of the briefest and most-cited in the history of literary theory. As Barthes maintains, the author is a *scriptor*, his or her function is the production, not explanation, of a text. Explaining would be to restrict a text's meaning, and a text's meaning resides in language, the way language works on a reader—it has nothing to do with the author or authorial intention, his or her identity, nationality, ethnicity, the historical context, and so forth. In his essay "What Is an Author?" Michel Foucault asserts that not all writers are authors, but that all authors are writers. The author's performance of the authorial function is part of the text, but irrelevant to the interpretative process. Both Barthes and Foucault adhere to the thesis that the author is language, that is, that language is the author.

Whatever the case may be, perhaps more than ever before, contemporary *writers* cling to their symbolic authorial thrones with all their might, desperately self-identifying as *authors*. It could be that their anxiety is provoked by the plethora of new terms such as creative writer and creative writing, which presuppose the existence of uncreative writers, uncreative writing—and, God forbid—an uncreative imagination. The implied existence of both "creative" and "uncreative" writing, each being equally valid, is particularly hard for "creative writers" to accept. The dawn of the digital future has only increased the author/writer confusion—just think of the fan fiction phenomenon and collaborative writing projects; the attempts to establish collective authors and authorships; the popularity of self-publishing, internet novels, cell-phone novels, twitterature; the new flabbiness of the very concept of literature; the attendant de-canonization and re-canonization; the re-semantification of plagiarism and intellectual property; the culture of remix, and copy and paste; the changes wrought as the publishing industry tries to adapt to new technology; the surge of "amateurism," and the concurrent flood of "professional" education, i.e., creative writing programs.

Ideas about "the death of the author" might still sound alluring in the texts of Barthes and Foucault, yet the literary context in which they were born has long been aborted. Our time is completely different, and brutally so. When someone steals the title of one of your books and uses it as her own, even gets in touch to let you know what she's done—expectant of your blessing—and when you refuse, she accuses you of being overly sensitive about matters of intellectual property, as an author, it's there, right there, your enthusiasm for any theoretical burial of the author and authorship wanes.

Do two people inhabit the body of he or she who works with the pen? The first, a diligent, self-deprecating hand worker, or "crafter of texts," the second, his or her media persona, the "author"? Are readers co-authors? And if so, does only an "author" need readers, or does a "crafter of texts" need them too? In this rather promiscuous relationship, how do we assign authorship roles? If the author died forty years ago (as theorists claim), but is not yet buried, and has in fact been resurrected (as literary practitioners suggest), perhaps he or she should be issued a temporary ID card? But in which register should the author be entered—that of the living, the dead, or the resurrected?

The title of this essay was inspired by a question my young niece posed to me. She didn't know what the word "author" meant, so as a diversion inquired, "What's an author made of then?" And indeed, let's start with that one—what *is* an author made of?

NAME

Starbucks is a kind of instant psychotherapy, boosting our self-confidence together with our caffeine levels. At Starbucks we buy a personalized little treat, a coffee that is ours and ours alone, because they even write our name on it.

When a bouncy young Starbucks barista asked me my name for the first time, I articulated it with conviction and clarity.

"Say what?!"

"Du-brav-ka," I repeated.

"Say whaaaat?!"

I said it again, and then again, just louder. The people in line behind me were already bitching. A short while later, a plastic cup with "Dwbra" scribbled on it arrived. I relayed the episode to a countryman who lives in Los Angeles, where my Starbucks initiation had occurred. That was twenty years ago.

"Jesus, what a dumbass! Who told you you've got to give your own name?!"

To be honest, it hadn't occurred to me not to.

"I always say Tito!" he fired.

"And?"

"And nothing. I just love hearing: Titoooo, your coffee's reaaaadyyyy!"

I took his advice and tried using Marx and Engels, but the Starbucks crew didn't quite get the message I was sending. In the end I chose a regular name. At Starbucks, I'm Jenny.

I learned my lesson: if I want coffee, I have to adapt, my personality has to conform. The barista's ear only hears what it's given to hear, and that's Jenny. This is a story about authors and authorship. If an author wants visibility—and we all do—he or she has to adjust his or her general tone, it has to be a tone discernable to the imaginary ear of the populace at large. Jenny is a collection of vowels and consonants everyone hears. "Dwbra" is not. I know this. I've tested it out in many parts of the world.

Hmmm, "general tone," what I do mean by that? The general tone is the context, and the context is dictated by the dominant literature, inevitably that of the predominant language, which is, at least currently, English. Our context is thus an Anglo-American one. What about other great literatures? Statistics confirm the jawdropping fact that European countries translate significant numbers of

American and British authors, yet translations make up barely three percent of Anglo-American publishing. Viewed in this light, the tastes of the German, Croatian, French, Swedish, Dutch, and other reading publics, are in many ways pre-formed, their ears attuned to "Jenny," not "Dwbra." Yet as we know, "Jenny" and "Dwbra" might be the same person, the same literary text, just with two different names. If the substance is the same, why is one text readable, the other unreadable; one heard, the other not; one visible, the other invisible? Why do the Dutch scuttle to the bookstore the minute the Booker Prize winner is announced, yet local literary prizes leave them cold? Why did Croatian journalists scribble long obituaries to Christopher Hitchens, when Hitchens's books have never been translated into Croatian (and few have even heard of him), yet a rare Croatian literary success abroad is glossed in a few reluctant lines?

Even when passing myself off as "Jenny," communication at Starbucks still has its limits. In a Dublin Starbucks I recently had the following exchange:

"Name?"

"Jenny . . ."

"How are we today, Jenny?"

"Good, thanks."

"It's grand to be good, is it not, Jenny . . . "

The kid had clearly passed Starbucks's customer service training, and it was obviously centered on the mind-numbing repetition of my name.

"Here's your coffee, Jenny . . ."

"Thanks," I said, taking a seat at one of the high chairs at the bar.

"What are your plans for the day, Jenny?" the kid asked.

"To hang myself . . ."

"Good choice, Jenny . . ." he replied, his tone of voice unchanged, and served the next customer.

This wee episode illustrates that even as Jenny I still have to accept a standardized form of communication if I want potential readers (and Starbucks's employees!) to actually hear me, and continue engagement. Because if the global marketplace has undergone McDonaldsification and Starbucksification, if Apple stores, the modern temples of our times, are erected in the most prominent places in our cities, tens of thousands of people circulating through them on a daily basis, then why wouldn't all other human activities—religion, politics, cinema, television, literature—behave in line with the same market principles, as mega-nodes of standardization? Participants in the market—authors, producers, consumers—all have to master the language of McDonalds, Starbucks, Apple, whomever. Like it or not, it means that I have to be "Jenny." If by some rare stroke of luck I manage to penetrate the sound barrier as "Dwbra," I might even enjoy a slight advantage over "Jenny," because people might then show greater tolerance for my disrespect of the codes of standard communication. She's "Dwbra," they'll say, she's *culturally incomprehensible*. That's the sort of comment Amazon's online "executors" make, ventriloquists for the genes of the thousands of executors who throughout history got off on their secret duty. Even today it's a secret one, the difference being that thanks to the Internet, anyone can execute in secrecy. I mean, how the hell would I know who the jerk-off hiding behind the "Batman" avatar is? His comment on one of my books: "something Slavic, completely incomprehensible."

Those with whom I live in "promiscuity"—my "co-authors," publishers, editors, booksellers, readers, critics, even "Batman"—beckon me not toward compromise (which would be a violation of my authorial autonomy), but the standardization of my message; its form, volume, language, meaning, tone, the puissance of its tone . . . Whether I want to stay "Dwbra" or become "Jenny," to attempt total or superficial transformation, to submit to standardized communication or remain "coffee-less"—it's entirely up to me. That I bear the consequences of my decisions is self-evident, and the results are plain to see.

GENDER

I was once a literary guest of a gregarious West European mayor. There was a group of us, writers, invited to dinner at a majestic table in the banquet room of a grand city hall. Stooped under the weight of his chains, the mayor entertained us with a potted history of the city and its most famous denizens. Their oil portraits peered down on us from the banquet room walls, visually underscoring the historical tour. As my gaze slid across the portraits—the shoes with raised heels, the ribbons and bows on manly feet, the tight satin trousers and puffy turkey-like jowls, mini and massive moustaches, wigs and frilly collars, walking sticks and gloves, hats, feathers, and rings—the thought occurred to me as clear as the figures on a cash register: Look at them, they're all men!

It was an epiphany that worked like a jammed trigger, my brain automatically becoming a montage table on which I assembled shots of similar portraits, similar sculptures of commanders-in-chief and generals, similar images of poets and thinkers, folk leaders and politicians, kings and tsars, fire-fighters and hunters, policemen and soldiers. At breakneck speed my brain pumped out book covers, newspaper headlines, encyclopedia entries, television clips, cinematic fragments . . . unbelievable, all full of men! Suddenly—just like the indelible Mr. "Everything comes from India" from the BBC series *Goodness Gracious Me!* who claims that everything in the world is Indian—it really was raining men, though none were Indian. Looking at Da Vinci's *The Last Supper*, the intransigent Mr. "Everything . . ." persists in claiming the painter is Indian, the picture "Indian," and when asked why, he replies: "No women!" Hasn't gender discrimination become invisible precisely because it is so obvious and so incredibly pervasive? Why are West European and North American women scandalized (if indeed they really are) by the discrimination endured by their "sisters" in Asia or Africa, yet simultaneously fail to see that they themselves live in a gender-discriminating world? Do none of them see it, or have they all simply capitulated and beat their retreat?

The city hall episode isn't the most judicious of examples, I can admit that. It's hard to believe powerful moments of cognition occur smack bang in the middle of city halls, and it's harder still to believe that the realization is hitting me again at this very moment (*Hey, sister, where you been all your life?!*). Yet it is equally unbelievable to think that men and women are, at any given moment, conscious of the dictates of gender in both their professional lives, and in life in general; that every move they make is not guided by this consciousness. In literary life, this consciousness usually strikes by stealth, like a betrayal, a knife in the back, inevitably so torturous we immediately erase it or fob it off for another day (*Ah, I'll think about it tomorrow!*). But tomorrow we delete it all again, fatalistically reconciling ourselves with the order of things, each of us alone, as lonely as a samurai. "Things are the way they are," we say, playing blind man's bluff, ready to swallow the insult, marching on, tormented by the same anxiety—the anxiety of authorship—that forever begs mastery anew. Saddest of all, and psychologically the most interesting, the exclusion of women is inevitably accompanied by the silence of other women, who lack the will to intervene.

In contrast to most women, the vast majority of men feel very comfortable in the literary world. Literature is their territory, they're well "at home"; literature is their armchair, their pair of slippers, their pipe to smoke. The history of literature is the history of men—poets, novelists, dramatists, essayists, thinkers, philosophers; it's friends and *buddies*, talking heads and fellow players, idols and inspirations. Literature is an extended male family. Although female authors have participated in *professional* literary life for some *two centuries*,[1] they're still classed as arrivistes, immigrants, and stowaways. Most men mentally address their work to other men, and most women address theirs to men too. Literature is a man's playing field, men jockey for the ball; women can only sit on the sidelines and cheer. Of course, male "players" don't have anything against women, they're just not that interested in them; most often, women simply aren't in their field of vision. Men can't conceive of sharing the turf with women, but sure, they're welcome as cheerleaders.

---

1 Irrespective of my own early participation in professional literary life, the historical record shows that women have been consistently erased from the public domain, from professional organizations and institutions of canonization (national academies, school reading lists, histories of literature, and so forth). In mid-nineteenth century America, books by women made up half the bestseller lists. Critical opinion soon formed evaluatory codes for "women's writing." Women were tasked with domestic subjects such as children and the family, with matters of religion and morality, their texts aesthetically crowned or dismissed in accordance with how well they satisfied the burdens of gender expectations—in other words, the extent to which they conformed. Women didn't create this division of labor, men did. How might we otherwise explain terms such "lady author," "authoress," "poetess," or "criticess," all ironically coined to describe women in literature?

On the literary playing field, the "cheerleaders" include translators, librarians, editors, agents, studious critics (of the male oeuvre), archivists. Isn't it best we all work where we're most at home? Men feel at ease in literature, they're masters of polemicizing among themselves, backscratching and backbiting, appearing in public together, critiquing each other, devising little strategies, swimming in formations like dolphins, forming literary clans, backslapping each other, savaging each other—and all the while they mentally hold each other's hands, as men in some regions do in real life. This collegial intimacy is sometimes so overpowering that they refer to their literary *buddies* by first or nick names, smug in the assumption that their readers and audiences will know who they're on about.

Female writers remain invisible until they speak the language of pornography, or the language of money, the "male tongue." Then they dominate the bestseller lists. Asked who inspires her, current dominatrix E. L. James rattled off names of women writers who plough similar territory, sending out a clear message in the process: In the literary world of financial profit, women hold pole position—their idols and inspiration "sisterly" writers, the millions who deliriously consume their products, also women.

The question of whether what E. L. James writes is literature, and if it's not, then what *is* literature, is today completely irrelevant. "If literature has died, literary activity continues with unabated, if not increased vigor," wrote Alvin Kernan in his long-forgotten *The Death of Literature*. The word literature is bidding its farewell to everyday language use, and trundling along with it are critical frames of reference and the very language of criticism. New terms are now in circulation: the *publishing industry*, the *writing industry*. What the writing industry intends to call the worker or "direct producer" remains to be seen. Maybe the current appellation of "content provider" will prevail.

If women rule the bestseller lists, men remain firmly seated in the first rows of so-called "serious" literature. At least that's how it is in the Yugozone, in the literatures of the former Yugoslavia. Once friends, for a time political enemies, Yugozone writers are now *buddies* again. Not only do the "brothers" stick tight when among their own, they also click together like magnets in "fraternal" multi-ethnic and multi-national formations (a Serb and a Croat, a Croat and a Montenegrin, a Montenegrin and a Serb, all together with a Bosnian or an Albanian, you get the picture). Why is male bonding so attractive in the literary world? For two reasons: The first is ineluctably socio-biological (even male dolphins swim in formations!), the second purely financial. In any case, these are the very tendencies supported by the cultural structures of the European Union, which understands culture as a sedative for calming inter-ethnic tensions, as a kind of yoga, a means of transport (cultural exchange, etc.), a bridge (that links nations), as a diplomatic strategy (culture knows no borders), as a potential tourism windfall, as everything and anything. Writers themselves have done the math and the figures don't lie: The new national markets (Croatian, Serbian, Bosnian, and Montenegrin) are simply too small. And who would have thought—the language of those literatures is the same after all!

With the advent of new media, public displays of male literary affection have blossomed into a genre. Affectionate email exchanges between two writers, TV appearances (a writerly coupling or three-some with a friendly brother in the middle, a hostess taking on the fraternal foursome); live appearances (a team of buddies performing);

essays on autobiographical "bromances," they're all irreducibly male genres. And what of the female role in these fraternal literary relationships? As the brothers conclude tapping the veins of each other's wisdom, a woman's name will suddenly bleed out. "Say hi to Cica!" "And you say hi to Mica!" Cica and Mica are the brothers' partners.

Stumbling across this kind of literary "material," foreigners might think it the spawn of Balkan blood brotherhoods, or else a special kind of homoerotic Balkan soft-porn. Thank God this "material" almost never makes it beyond the borders of the Yugozone, so no one thinks about it at all. But if the material did indeed find legs, it could be that people in other parts of the world would think it completely natural, little different to what they've already seen among their own. Let's not forget, men mentally hold each other's hand *everywhere*, it's just here and there they hold hands for real. I mean, who was it that hustled their way into Rembrandt's famous picture? Those who had the money to buy a ticket to eternity: the boys, the buddies, the "night-watchmen," the "Indians."

It's enough to do a little google of the most important European literary prizes, to click on the rubric "previous winners," and the humiliating evidence speaks for itself. One of the most significant annual European prizes for contribution to European culture, society, and social science (a prize awarded by one of the most declaratively tolerant and democratic European states) is this year celebrating its sixtieth anniversary. In the sixty years of its existence, a woman has won the prize once. The fact that one year the prize was shared by three men and a woman (her name was Marguerite Yourcenar), and another year went to a married couple, is hardly a corrective. The result (59-to-1) reveals one of two possible things: Either women are mentally backward, which would explain men's absolute intellectual supremacy, or women are systematically exposed to chronic professional discrimination. Maybe professional discrimination is but a form of that "ontological lack" that men—in possession of that infamous appendage—have foisted upon women as an enduring physical failing and inadequacy.

I admit that of late I've developed an unpleasant involuntary neurosis: Everything I set eyes on, everything I touch, I immediately put through my internal calculator, working out the ratio of men to women. I take everything in via a gender-based numerical screen: literary magazines, newspapers, feuilletons, literary production, scholarly articles, reviews, literary prizes, the lot. Courtesy of this involuntary neurosis I can say with an enormous degree of confidence that even a completely marginal human endeavor such as literature destroys every illusion about gender equality. Literature is *Indian* too!

As far as my neurosis goes, I'm not alone; other women are also prone to numerical mania. Bidisha, an English writer, novelist, and feminist has observed the keen paradox: the more women in literature, the more they're invisible. Bidisha defines the professional discrimination of women in literature as "the erasure of women from public life," which she abbreviates as "femicide." "Discrimination is obvious," says Bidisha, "all you have to do is count."[2]

If the issue really is femicide, why is it that women have such a hard time raising their voices, are too reluctant to unite, to seek the support of other women in their profession? I once met an international

---

2   Bidisha, "I'm tired of being the token woman," *The Guardian*, April 22 2010.

feminist icon at a conference. She christened me a "Croatian aboriginal," telling me how she'd just returned from a summer holiday in Croatia and how she'd watched "Croatian aboriginal women" feed rucola to pigs, which in her view was unbearably barbaric. On another occasion, an intellectual goddess lost her cool when I failed to display the requisite level of humility and gratitude at one of my books being published in a major world language. In fact, I'd shown ingratitude and insolence by daring remark that the honorarium I'd received for the book was humiliatingly modest (which, naturally, it was). Both women conversed with me the way a former servant converses with a present slave. I haven't the least intention of drawing any groundbreaking conclusion from the two incidents, yet the truth remains that the gender question and the professional discrimination of women provokes unhealthy reactions among both genders of the writer's guild. My male colleagues tend not to understand the problem; my female colleagues tend to refuse to understand it.

If literature is dead, if the author is dead, if literary theory and criticism are dead—all of which the literary Jedi Masters assure us— why do literary little boys refuse to surrender half the literary galaxy to their legally entitled sisters?

NATIONALITY

At a social gathering in Berlin I once met a Roma community representative, a fellow countryman. I say *representative* because the guy held a position of importance in a European Roma association. Our common homeland had fallen apart, the savagery in Bosnia continued apace, and I had made my way abroad, but still didn't have anywhere I might call home. At a given moment I think every immigrant feels like an orphan, although most never admit it. In any case, even if I meant it more in jest than in seriousness—or,

who knows, maybe it was a serious thing said in jest—in a moment
of weakness I blubbered out . . .

"Couldn't you Berlin Roma take me under your wing?"

"What do you mean?"

"You could 'adopt' me, declare me a Roma writer . . ."

"Eh, sister, that's a no-go . . ." said the Roma representative.

"Why not then?"

"Well, for a start, you're not Roma!"

I don't know why I thought the Roma—easily the most discriminated against ethnic minority in Europe—might be receptive to the
idea. But on the subject of rejection, I've had a few of those in my
life, and they keep coming. It's a no-go, sister, you're not a Croat.
No way, sister, you're not a Serb. Forget it, sister, you're not Bosnian,
you're not even American. Oh c'mon, sister, you're not Dutch. It's
not that I'm especially pushy; people just like putting the boot in.

Hey, Slavs was the national anthem of the country where I was
born.[3] Having repeated the words so many times, I should know
them by heart, but I don't. I was never able to remember them.
There were so many occasions, from primary school on into adult-
hood, when we'd rise from our seats and open our mouths like fish,
half-speaking along. The words remain a mystery to me to this day,
but they start with something about grandfathers and sons (*Hey,
Slavs, our grandfathers' spirits burn bright / so long as sons' hearts beat
for the nation*). Then a collective voice tells an invisible listener that

---

3   The hymn, *Hey, Slovaks*, was written by Samuel-Samo Tomašik, a Slovak.
In the spirit of the pan-Slavic movement of the time, he ended up dedicat-
ing the song to all Slavs, and in 1848 it was sung at the pan-Slavic congress
in Prague. A hundred years later, Yugoslavs "adopted" Tomašik's song as the
official Yugoslav national anthem.

the Slavic spirit will endure for the ages (*the Slavic spirit will live on / endure for the ages*), irrespective of the fact that it's threatened by catastrophes such as the *abyss of hell* and the *roar of thunder*. The collective Slavic spirit calls forth the storm to swallow all in its wake, for an earthquake to crack stone and shatter wood (*May the storm rip the sky / may the stone crack, the trees split asunder / may the earth quake*). In this climatic drama the Slavs stand as resolutely as cliff faces, like extras in a cinematic biblical spectacle. But filming was wrapped up long ago and everyone's gone home, apart from the Slavs who are still standing there, probably waiting for someone to tell them they're also free to go. And then, like a thunderbolt in a clear sky, the line *damned be the traitor to his homeland!* rings out. The damned traitor's identity remains a mystery—it's only natural catastrophes giving the Slavs hell. My guess is that the traitor is anyone with a ticket in his or her pocket, the coward who refuses to live in a country threatened by the abyss of hell and the roar of thunder, anyone who doesn't find life as a cliff face particularly exciting. The traitor could be the extra who first remembers to go home, on whose head the terrifying curse *damned be the traitor to his homeland!* rains down.

It's easy to be wise in retrospect, but when you repeat lines like these for a good part of your schooling, they're definitely what we might call formative. The melody—the medium carrying the message—gives you goosebumps to this day, yet the content remains as hazy as ever. The Croatian anthem, *Our Beautiful Homeland*, is no better, and though it only cherry-picks a few verses from the full version of the song, it's still longer than the Yugoslav anthem. Regardless of the fact it was written almost two hundred years ago (in 1835), its verses are eerily reminiscent of a tourism promo clip, the kind countries make for the Eurovision Song Contest—jump shots of mountains, waterways, wheat fields, and similar telegenic material. The anthem's buzzwords are "glory," "unique," and "fearless," and there's even a little gothic detail about ancestors who bypass their graves and go straight to heaven, the family tomb apparently a favourite Croatian picnic spot. As the anthem dates from a time before telecommunication networks, the maritime Croat implores the sea to send a message out to the world that *a Croat loves his homeland.*

To me, the words of every anthem and every prayer border on the incomprehensible, which is how they were intended. The tribal shamans, the religious fathers of the people, they all know that the communal chanting and vacuous repetition of an incomprehensible text only increases its magical power. As systems of authority, the institutions of homeland and church harness fuzzy language and the melodic release of vocal cords to dazzle their subjects; citizens, worshippers, whomever.

Although it's dependent on the situation, the trouble and merriment really begin when the three "Ps" get together, when the Politician and the Priest get their other buddy, the Poet, to sing along. Let's be frank here, the Poet is the weakest link, and can be drummed from the holy trinity at the Priest or Politician's whim. Many writers have described the intoxication of belonging (to a home, a homeland, a country, a faith) and the trauma of unbelonging. Thomas Mann treats the latter in *Tonio Kröger,* particularly in the masterly episode where Kröger, having returned to his birthplace after a thirty-year absence, is given the third degree by a local cop who thinks him a suspicious *individual.* The proofs of a forthcoming book are insufficient evidence that this *individual,* who claims to be a writer, might belong to the race of blue-eyed and blond-haired victors, those who no one ever looks up or down.

Why is the Poet set on ingratiating himself with the Politician and Priest? It's because they're all honey-tongued buddies, a trio well-versed in promising the people a brighter tomorrow. The poet may well be a "linguistic magician," a "nightingale," an "engineer of human souls," but aren't the Priest and the Politician too? They too sell illusions, and like the Poet, their power resides in the ability to win over a crowd. The Poet is the nation's old school PR man, which goes some way toward explaining why small nations so rabidly appoint poets their ambassadors, and, not infrequently, their presidents. If the Poet discharges his duties with distinction, he'll be generously rewarded; if by some slip of the tongue he profanes his country and her honor (and thus that of the Priest and the Politician) he might end up in prison, in exile, in anonymity . . . Bad options no doubt, but options nonetheless.

All in all, the alliance of the Politician, Priest, and Poet is complex, historically rich, dramatic, exciting, often fatal, and inevitably—unavoidable. Even if the Poet eventually wins his freedom, no longer requiring the assistance of Priest or Politician, it's no matter, the two of them will then go to him. Just think of the honorary doctorates bestowed on J. K. Rowling, all the politicians who have curtsied in her direction. Sure, she curtsies too, though she doesn't have to. Accused of promoting witchcraft and magic over religion in her work, Rowling responded: "I believe in God, not magic!" The Priest breathed a contented sigh of relief—he doesn't like competition.

Having a certain Felix Landau, an SS officer in Drohobych, as a fan of his sketches saved Bruno Schulz's life for a time. Landau made him his "personal Jew," hiring him to paint his son's room. One "black Thursday," on a day when 250 Jews were killed in Drohobych, Bruno Schulz was felled by the bullet of SS officer Karl

Günther. Günther shot Schulz as revenge on Landau for having shot his own "personal Jew," a dentist. At least that's how legend has it. Today three states jostle to incorporate Schulz in the fabric of their national culture: Poland (because Schulz wrote in Polish), Israel (for obvious reasons), and Ukraine (because Drohobych is today in western Ukraine). About twenty years ago there was a scandal when a mural Schulz painted for his temporary protector was found. Sections of the mural were promptly whisked off to Israel and installed in Yad Vashem. The Ukrainian Ministry of Culture confirmed that it had donated the mural to Yad Vashem because in return Yad Vashem had promised to fund the construction of a Schulz museum in Drobobych. Schulz's fate—one of the saddest and most ironic of literary fates—illustrates the extent to which the Poet is always a plaything, putty in the hands of Politician and Priest, even after his death (which they of course ably concealed). Priest and Politician never miss a chance to "warm" themselves on a book either.

As far as writers, their nationalities, and their countries of residence go, things aren't always in accord, don't always match expectations. Some writers change countries and languages, chance sends one to a hospitable country, another some place less hospitable, but most writers stick to the countries where they were born. Being a writer is complicated enough. Yet being an Anglo-American writer and being a Malaysian one isn't quite the same thing, just as being an Anglo-American woman writer among Anglo-American male writers is not the same thing—nor, for that matter, is being a Malaysian woman writer within Malaysian literature and being one on the world literary map. Wanting to mark his or her territory on the literary map, a Malaysian has to display vastly greater talent and invest vastly greater energy than his or her Anglo-American colleague. There's no mystery in the power relations. For a great writer, a small country lacking a significant literary tradition is a great misfortune. Had he been a German writer, Miroslav Krleža would today tower on the world literary map as one of its peaks. But Miroslav Krleža only exists on Croatian maps. Minor writers are in much better shape—if it weren't for their small countries and languages, many writers wouldn't be able to call themselves such. Small countries tend to seek out literary representatives cut to their own size; they wouldn't know what to do with a great writer, a minor one suits all concerned. For a minor writer, the backing of his small country is his most potent weapon.

The global marketplace is particularly enamored with the idea of homelands, nations, and nationalities; there is, after all, good money to be made. At the apotheosis of modernism, Virginia Woolf declared, "As a woman I have no country. As a woman I want no country. As a woman, my country is the whole world." To me, it seems a declaration that was then as equally "incomprehensible" as it is today. Because literature—as an exemplar of a nation's "spiritual wealth," as a "bridge between peoples" (alongside the many other characteristics attributed to it)—is also a form of ethno-business. Unfortunately. And one sometimes gets the impression that many writers are awfully adroit in the role of ethno-businessmen.

THE AUTHOR: DEAD AND ALIVE

> *Those who say the author is dead usually have in mind to rifle his wardrobe.*
>
> —*Les Murray*[4]

---

4   The citation is from Andrew Bennett's *The Author* (Routledge, 2005), one of the most instructive studies on the subject of the author and authorship.

In a single sentence, poet Les Murray nonchalantly casts aside the manifold efforts of his "natural" allies—critics, literary theorists, and literary historians—and their responses to one of the most complex literary questions, that of the author and authorship. And if I zip the mouth of the literary theorist in me shut, and let the writer speak, at least fleetingly I have to agree with him.

Although there is, as yet, no accord among literary historians on who or what gave birth to the author and when—whether it was the advent of written culture or the invention of publishing (i.e., legal regulation in book production)—the author, it seems, is already dead. Having established himself and become an institution in the nineteenth century, by the mid-twentieth century his relevance was already in question. The institution of the author and authorship was actually tragi-comically brief; richer and lengthier by far is the story of anonymous literary creation.[5]

Yet theorists such as Barthes, Foucault, Terry Eagleton, or Pierre Bourdieu didn't bury the author; one can't even credit the scribes who periodically proffer hegemonic, universalist (male, naturally), white (*we can't worry about the whole world!*), West European and North American (*the Arabs are loaded, they can look after themselves!*) thinking on literature, literary values, and the author and authorship. As we know, the author is a kind of social consensus, as is literature itself; the author is a mutant adapting to the demands and expectations of the purchaser, irrespective of who this might be—king, tsar, state, religious community, imagined literary public, social class, or market. There is no author without social consensus.

---

5   See John Mullan's most interesting study, *Anonymity: A Secret History of English Literature* (Princeton University Press, 2008).

If you don't believe this, try explaining you're an author to the Brazilian Awa tribe.

The institution of literature, at least as we have hitherto known it, is disintegrating by the day, and is doing so together with the foundations on which its construction rests. The Author is one of the key elements, the traditional author, that is. Because in today's celebrity culture, authors are more worried about how they might create an authorial public persona than, for example, the narrative masks of their novels. It's the authorial persona that sells books, or so we're told. This explains why in terms of self-representation, on websites, in the brief biographical notes on inside covers, we see those clumsy collections of words attempting to confirm the identity of the person in question: *novelist, essayist, author of such and such.* Don't *novelist* and *essayist* also automatically imply the concept of *authorship*? Or is the word *author* itself a kind of bonus medal, which we award ourselves (or is awarded to us by others) in the belief it might seal our social standing? Maybe the word *author* is just a symptom of a deep internal fear that we are all together going to disappear, swept away by the first strong gust of a new cultural wind?

Most people associate "visual art" with strong ("scandalous") authorial personas, Damien Hearst being a case in point. Building his or her authorial personae—conscious that they live in the celebrity culture that is ours, a modern version of polytheism—many artists, consciously or unconsciously use self-beatification, self-divinization (one of the forms of canonization in celebrity culture), and thus exploit the religious potential of the artistic act. It's how Marina Abramović turned MoMA into Međugorje (or Lourdes), herself into Our Lady, and thousands of visitors into believers and pilgrims for the duration of her three-month project, "The Artist Is Present."

Dressed as the Virgin Mary full of grace, Abramović lowered her healing gaze onto visitors, flickered her eyelids, and occasionally let a tear fall from her eye. Reporting that they had undergone a cathartic experience, many visitors also shed tears. It turns out that today's celebrated authors are indeed modern saints, with devotees who follow in the footsteps of their teacher, cementing his or her canonical place on the artistic map of the world, spreading his or her artistic vision. At the same MoMA exhibition, young per-formers and devotees of Abramović's artistic teachings reactivated her early performance works, in the self-same way that groups of amateur faithful perform the nativity scene at Christmas, or more masochistic Catholics tread Jesus's path to Calvary. The repetition of Abramović's performances by younger artists was in the service of the canonization of the authorial persona of Marina Abramović, not the affirmation of a particular form of artistic expression, in this case, performance art. Moreover, the repetition of a live artistic act, such as performance art, is in contradiction with the very essence and purpose of the form. Repeated, performance art becomes an artistic souvenir. When an anonymous young visitor to Abramović's MoMA show did her own little Pussy Riot and undressed—an attempt to display her devotion to the great artist—the museum guards immediately led her away. Why? Because the heathen have never been allowed to act out any instinct that might disturb the reli-gious ritual, in this case that of self-beatification. But then, Marina Abramović is a woman and an artist, aware of the powerful world of stereotypes, and her own position within it. Women artists are rarely canonized and even more rarely proclaimed saints. Conscious of this, Abramović decided to take matters into her own hands.

Buying a book by Haruki Murakami, many readers throughout the world first and foremostly buy entry to the heaving mass of fans of this "literary saint," then they buy a story about global literary success, and then also into one about community. In the symbolic act of buying a book they create community with other readers throughout the world, a kind of spiritual pilgrimage. There, perhaps, lies the mystery of cultural conformism, the answer to the question of why most people buy the things most people buy.

The purchase of a symbolic, "spiritual" product (a book, film, album, video game, etc.) is actually contact with another consumer, the creation of belonging, the overcoming of loneliness. It is the principle, it seems, on which culture markets flourish, whether those of children, teenagers, adolescents, or adults . . .

The market, it seems, has no need for an original, romantic-style genius, but for an appropriately "off-the-rack" author, someone who in the celebrity culture in which we live will substitute excellence and genius with an authorial persona, an essence coupled with good design. Because it appears the author expired the moment the idea of the "mad genius" and the "singularity of the artistic act" were expunged from the social consensus, the populist idea of "stand in line and have your shot" taking their place. Beda Foltin, the hero of Karel Čapek's final, unfinished novel *The Composer Foltin*, would today not incite the moral opprobrium he did in the time the novel was set. Foltin, who fancies himself a talented composer and goes about stealing others' motifs to create an opera he calls *Judith* (a musical Frankenstein), would simply be dissed as a crap DJ. In a culture of remix, cut and paste, computer programs, fan fiction and the people who write it, twitter, cell-phone novels, self-publishing, and anonymous authors and editors, a culture in which the absolute absence of responsibility prevails, Čapek's moral message would be met by general incomprehension.

One mystery, however, remains: Whence the urge in each of us to try our creative hand, to find *our* listeners, viewers, and readers? Whence the hatred and envy of those who achieve greater success than we do? The millions of frustrated individuals—writers, editors, painters, musicians, directors, the malicious creeps and sarcastic douche bags, the self-appointed censors and critics, the envious, the wannabe artists hungry for fame? And whence the righteous, convinced fame has unfairly passed them by, the copiers, imitators, plagiarists, self-appointed assessors of others' talent, the sickos fantasizing about their future masterpieces, the art lovers hiding penknives in their pockets, just waiting to slash an artist's canvas? Whence the millions of amateurs who plaster themselves all over the Internet, with their films, songs, sketches, their monologues on painting, literature, and philosophy, seeking attention and respect for the simple fact that they're there on our computer screens, in front of our noses, for the mere fact that they, well, exist? The terrifying armies of devotees and haters? The vicious jealousy of the creative act? Could it be because the creative work—at least as it stands in the current social contract—is a potential ticket to eternity; to a street bearing our name, a poem in a future anthology?!

"One of the books that caused great harm was James Joyce's *Ulysses*, which is pure style. There is nothing there. Stripped down, Ulysses is a twit." This was Brazilian global superstar Paulo Coelho's recent take. "I'm modern because I make the difficult seem easy, and so I can communicate with the whole world," he claimed.

The Peter Shaffer drama *Amadeus* (1979) and the Miloš Forman film of the same name (1984) rank among the most significant modern texts on the unbearable lightness of genius and the murderous

weight of envy. *Amadeus* is the story of Salieri and Mozart's puta-
tive rivalry, or more to the point, Salieri's maniacal obsession with
Mozart's genius, one that will drive Mozart to the grave, and Salieri
to madness. Six years older than Mozart, Salieri outlived him by
a full forty years. Antonio Salieri was the director of the Italian
opera at the Habsburg court, an esteemed European opera "man-
ager" (Vienna, Rome, Paris), a popular composer of his time, the
Austrian emperor's *Kapellmeister*, a music teacher and "coach" to
many greats, Franz Schubert, Ludwig van Beethoven, and Franz
Liszt among them. His music disappeared with his death. Thanks
to Shaffer's drama, and more so, Forman's film, Antonio Salieri has
undergone a modest artistic rehabilitation. Every year his hometown
of Legnago organizes the Salieri Opera Festival, the local theater
even bearing his name. Academic interest in his work has generated
demand for its performance: Here and there his operas are returning
to repertoires. So yeah, Salieri was an author, and Mozart was an
author. Who knows, maybe future generations won't be able to tell
the difference between the two. Or maybe they will, but simply
won't care.

History, cultural history too, heaves with ironic turns. Is the platitude about the inevitable triumph of artistic justice to be believed?
Questions of justice are usually settled by the victor's hand. In this
light, it's entirely possible that James Joyce will one day figure in a
Paulo Coelho biography as a footnote, with Joyce glossed as a minor
Irish writer who once wrote a book Paulo Coelho determined had
done great harm to literature. We don't really believe that something of the sort might happen, but not because James Joyce is an
Irish cultural icon, but rather because he's a golden goose for Irish
tourism. Whatever the case, that fact remains that the untalented

are feistier than the talented, the stupid feistier than the smart, the evil feistier than the good, that parasites outlive the body on which they feed, blood donors often bleed to death—and only vampires live forever.

ON-ZONE

Merhan Karimi Nasseri, an Iranian better known as Sir Alfred, lived at Charles de Gaulle Airport from 1998 until 2006, and for much of this time was a kind of tourist attraction. Steven Spielberg's 2004 film The Terminal *was in part inspired by Nasseri's life story. In contrast to Tom Hanks's character in the film, Alfred spent most of his time reading. "It's like a day at the library," he said.*

1.

A few years ago at Bucharest Airport I spotted a sign saying *Zona fumatore*, which simply means a smoking area—it just sounds way better in Romanian. You see all kinds of zones on your travels: free zones (*zona franca*), no-go zones, duty-free zones, you name it. West Germans used to call East Germany *die Zone*, by which they meant the Soviet Zone. There are time zones, erogenous zones, even Andrei Tarkovsky's *Stalker* is set in a zone. There's a weight-loss diet called The Zone, and then you've also got zoning, in the sense of urban planning. In sci-fi, a zone is usually some sort of dystopia. Hearing the word "zone," our first association is a clearly defined space, our second, its evanescence. Zones can be erected and dissembled like tents, ephemeral. Last but not least, there's a form of literary life we might call the "out-of-nation zone," best abbreviated as the ON-zone. I know a person who lives in that zone. That person is me.

I write in the language of a small country. I left that small country twenty years ago in an effort to preserve my right to a literary voice, to defend my writings from the constraints of political, national, ethnic, gender, and other ideological projections. Although true, the explanation rings a little phony, like a line from an intellectual soap opera. Parenthetically, male literary history is full of such lines, but with men being "geniuses," "rebels," "renegades," "visionaries," intellectual and moral bastions, etc.—when it comes to intellectual autobiographical kitsch, they get free passes. People only turn up their noses when it escapes a woman's lips. Even hip memes like "words without borders" and "literature without borders" ring pretty phony, too. The important point here is that having crossed the border, I found myself in a literary out-of-nation zone, the implications of which I only figured out much later.

It could be said that I didn't actually leave my country, but rather, that splitting into six smaller ones, my country left me. My mother tongue was the only baggage I took with me, the only souvenir my country bequeathed me. My spoken language in everyday situations was easy to switch, but changing my literary language, I was too old for that. In a second language I could have written books with a vocabulary of about five hundred words, which is about how many words million-shipping bestsellers have. Unfortunately, my ambitions lay elsewhere. I don't have any romantic illusions about the irreplaceability of one's mother tongue, nor have I ever understood the coinage's etymology. Perhaps this is because my mother was Bulgarian, and Bulgarian her mother tongue. She spoke flawless Croatian though, better than many Croats. On the off chance I did ever have any romantic yearnings, they were destroyed irrevocably almost two decades ago, when Croatian libraries were euphorically purged of "non-Croatian books," meaning books by Serbian writers, Croatian "traitors," books by "commies" and "Yugoslavs," books printed in Cyrillic. Mouths buttoned tight, my fellow writers bore witness to a practice that may have been short-lived, but was no less terrifying for it. The orders for the library cleansings came from the Croatian Ministry of Culture. Indeed, if I ever harbored any linguistic romanticism, it was destroyed forever the day Bosnian Serbs set their mortars on the National Library in Sarajevo. Radovan Karadžić, a Sarajevo psychiatrist and poet—a "colleague"—led the mission of destruction. Writers ought not forget these things. I haven't. Which is why I repeat them obsessively. For the majority of writers, a mother tongue and national literature are natural homes, for an "unadjusted" minority, they're zones of trauma. For such writers, the translation of their work into foreign languages is a kind of refugee shelter. And so translation is for me. In the euphoria of the Croatian bibliocide, my books also ended up on the scrap heap.

After several years of academic and literary wandering, I set up camp in a small and convivial European country. Both my former and my present literary milieu consider me a "foreigner," each for their own reasons of course. And they're not far wrong: I am a *foreigner*, and I have my reasons. The ON-zone is an unusual place to voluntarily live one's literary life. Life in the zone is pretty lonely, yet with the suspect joy of a failed suicide, I live with the consequences of a choice that was my own. I write in a language that has split into three—Croatian, Serbian, and Bosnian—but in spite of concerted efforts to will it apart, remains the same language. It's the language in which war criminals have pled their innocence at the Hague Tribunal for the past twenty years. At some point, the tribunals' tortured translators came up with an appropriate acronym: BCS (Bosnian-Croatian-Serbian). Understandably, the peoples reduced and retarded by their bloody divorce can't stand the fact that their language is now just an acronym. So the Croats call it Croatian, the Bosnians Bosnian, the Serbs Serbian, even the Montenegrins have come up with an original name: They call it Montenegrin.

What sane person would want a literary marriage with an evidently traumatized literary personality like me? No one. Maybe the odd translator. Translators keep me alive in literary life. Our marriage is a match between two paupers, our symbolic capital on the stock market of world literature entirely negligible. My admiration for translators is immense, even when they translate the names Ilf and Petrov as the names of Siberian cities. Translators are mostly humble folk. Almost invisible on the literary map, they live quiet lives in the author's shadow. My empathy with translators stems, at least in part, from my own position on the literary map; I often feel like I'm invisible too. However things really are, translating, even from a small language, is still considered a profession. But writing in a small language, from a literary out-of-nation zone, now that is not a profession—*that* is a diagnosis.

The platitude about literature knowing no borders isn't one to be believed. Only literatures written in major languages enjoy passport-free travel. Writerly representatives of major literatures travel without papers, a major literature their invisible *lettre de noblesse*. Writers estranged or self-estranged, exiled or self-exiled from their maternal literatures, they tend to travel on dubious passports. A literary customs officer can, at any time, escort them from the literary train under absolutely any pretext. The estranged or self-estranged female writer is such a rare species she's barely worth mentioning.

All these reasons help explain my internal neurosis: As an ON-writer I always feel obliged to explain my complicated literary passport to an imagined customs officer. And as is always the case when you get into a conversation with a customs officer on unequal footing, ironic multiplications of misunderstandings soon follow. What does it matter, you might say, whether someone is a Croatian, Belgian, or American writer? "Literature knows no borders," you retort. But it does matter: The difference lies in the reception of the author's position; it's in the way an imagined customs officer flicks through one's passport. And although it would never cross our minds to self-designate so, we readers—*we* are those customs officers!

Every text is inseparable from its author, and vice versa; it's just that different authors get different treatment. The difference is whether a text travels together with a male or female author, whether the author belongs to a major or minor literature, writes in a major or minor language; whether a text accompanies a famous or anonymous author, whether the author is young or old, Mongolian or English, Surinamese or Italian, an Arab woman or an American man, a homosexual or a heterosexual . . . All of these things alter the meaning of a text, help or hinder its circulation.

Let's imagine for a moment that someone sends me and a fellow writer—let's call him Dexter—to the North Pole to each write an essay about our trip. Let's also imagine a coincidence: Dexter and I return from our trip with exactly the *same* text. Dexter's position doesn't require translation, it's a universal one—Dexter is a representative of Anglo-American letters, the dominant literature of our time. My position will be translated as Balkan, post-Yugoslav, Croatian, and, of course, female. All told, a particular and specific one. My description of the white expanse will be quickly imbued with projected, i.e., invented, content. Customs officers will ask Dexter whether in the white expanse he encountered the metaphysical;

astounded that I don't live at "home," they'll ask me why I live in Amsterdam, how it is that I, of all people, got sent to the North Pole, and while they're at it, they'll inquire how I feel about the development of Croatian eco-feminism. Not bothering to read his work first, they'll maintain that Dexter is a great writer, and me, not bothering to read my work first either, they'll declare a kind of literary tourist guide—to the Balkan region, of course; where else?

To be fair, how my text about the North Pole will be received in my former literary community is also a question worth asking. As my encounter with the metaphysical? God no. Croats will ask me how the Croatian diaspora is getting on up there, how I—a Croatian woman—managed to cope in the frozen north, and whether I plunged a Croatian flag into the ice. Actually, in all likelihood my text won't even be published. With appropriate fanfare they'll publish Dexter's. It'll be called "How a great American writer warmed us to the North Pole."

That literature knows no borders is just a platitude. But it's one we need to believe in. Both originals and their translations exist in literature. The life of a translation is inseparable from the relatively stable life of its original, yet the life of a translation is often much more interesting and dramatic. Translations—poor, good, mangled, congenial—have rich lives. A reader's energy is interwoven in this life; in it are the mass of books that expand, enlighten, and entertain us, that "save our lives"; the books whose pages are imbued with our own experiences, our lives, convictions, the times in which we live, all kinds of things.

Many things can be deduced from a translation; and let us not forget, readers are also translators. *The Wizard of Oz*, for example, was my favorite children's book. Much later I found out that the book had traveled from the Russian to Yugoslavia and the rest of the East European world, and that it wasn't written by a certain A. Volkov (who had "adapted" it), but by the American writer Frank L. Baum. The first time I went to Moscow (way back in 1975) I couldn't shake the feeling that I had turned up in a monochrome Oz, and that I, like Toto, just needed pull back the curtain to reveal a deceit masked by the special effects of totalitarianism. Baum's innocent arrow pierced the heart of a totalitarian regime in a way the arrows of Soviet dissident literature never could.

Every translation is a miracle of communication, a game of Chinese Whispers, where the word at the start of the chain is inseparable from that exiting the mouth of whomever is at the end. Every translation is not only a multiplication of misunderstandings, but also a multiplication of meanings. Our lungs full, we need to give wind to the journey of texts, to keep watch for the eccentrics who send messages in bottles, and the equally eccentric who search for bottles carrying messages; we need to participate in the orgy of communication, even when it seems to those of us sending messages that communication is buried by the din, and thus senseless. Because somewhere on a distant shore a recipient awaits our message. To paraphrase Borges, he or she exists to misunderstand it and transform it into something else.

2.

According to data from the International Organization for Migration, the number of migrants has increased from 150 million in 2000 to an estimated 214 million today, meaning that migrants make up 3.1 percent of the world's population. Migrant numbers vary drastically from country to country: In Qatar, 87 percent of the population are migrants; in the UAE, 70 percent; Jordan, 46 percent; in Singapore, 41 percent. As a percentage, Nigeria, Romania, India, and Indonesia have the lowest numbers of migrants. Women make up 49 percent of the migrant population. Among the migrant population, 27.5 million are categorized as displaced persons, and 15.4 million as refugees. If all migrants were settled in a single state, it would be the fifth most populous in the world, after China, India, the U.S., and Indonesia, but ahead of Brazil. It's a fair assumption that in this imagined migrant state, there would be at least a negligible percentage of writers, half of whom would be women.

Writers who have either chosen to live in the ON-zone, or been forced to seek its shelter, need more oxygen than that provided by translations into foreign languages alone. For a full-blooded literary life, such writers need, inter alia, an imaginary library—a context in which their work might be located. Because more often than not, such work floats free in a kind of limbo. The construction of a context—of a literary and theoretical platform, a theoretical raft that might accommodate the dislocated and de-territorialized; the transnational and a-national; cross-cultural and transcultural writers; cosmopolitans, neo-nomads, and literary vagabonds; those who write in "adopted" languages, in newly-acquired languages, in multiple languages, in mother tongues in non-maternal habitats; all those who have voluntarily undergone the process of dispatriation[1]—much work on the construction of such a context remains.

---

1 "By dispatriation I mean the process of distancing oneself more from one's own native or primary culture than from one's own national identity, even if, as we have seen, in a many cases the two tend to coincide." Arianna Dagnino, "Transnational Writers and Transcultural Literature in the Age of Global Modernity," *Transnational Literature*, 4.2 (May 2012).

In *Writing Outside the Nation*,[2] some ten years ago Azade Seyhan attempted to construct a theoretical framework for interpreting literary works written in exile (those of the Turkish diaspora in Germany, for example), works condemned to invisibility within both the cultural context of a writer's host country (although written in German) and that of his or her abandoned homeland. This theoretical framework was transnational literature. In the intervening years, several new books have appeared,[3] and the literary practice of transnational literature has become increasingly rich and diverse. There are ever more young authors writing in the languages of their host countries: Some emigrated with their parents, and speak their mother tongue barely or not at all; others (for cultural and pragmatic, or literary and aesthetic reasons) have consciously exchanged their mother tongues for the language of their hosts. Some write in the language of their host countries while retaining the mental blueprint of their mother tongue, giving rise to surprising linguistic mélanges; others create defamiliarizing effects by mixing the vocabulary of two or sometimes multiple languages. Changes are afoot not only within individual texts, but also in their reception. The phenomenon of literary distancing is one I myself have experienced. Although I still write in the same language, I can't seem to follow contemporary Serbian, Croatian, and Bosnian literature with the ease I once did. I get hung up on things local readers wouldn't bat an eyelid at. I sense the undertones and nuances differently than they do, and it makes me wonder about the "chemical reaction" that

---

2 Princeton, NJ: Princeton University Press, 2001.

3 In addition to Seyhan's book, worth recommending are the edited collection *Transnationalism and Resistance: Experience and Experiment in Women's Writing*, edited by Adele Parker and Stephenie Young (Rodopi, 2013), and the collections, *The Creolization of Theory* (Duke UP, 2011), and *Minor Transnationalism* (Duke UP, 2005), edited by Françoise Lionnet, and Shu-mei Shih respectively.

takes place inside the recipient of a text (in this case, me) when cultural habitat, language, and addressee have all changed. My relationship toward the canonic literary values of the "region" has also changed. Texts I once embraced wholeheartedly now seem laughably weak. My own literary modus changed in the very moment I was invited to write a column for a Dutch newspaper. That was in 1992. I was temporarily in America, war raged in my "homeland," and the addressee of my columns was—a Dutch reader.

I don't know whether it's harder to articulate the ON-zone or to live it. Cultural mediators rarely take into account contemporary cultural practice, in which, at least in Europe, "direct producers" co-locate with a sizable cultural bureaucracy—from national institutions and ministries of culture, to European cultural institutions and cultural managers, to the manifold NGOs active in the sector. The cultural bureaucracy is primarily engaged in the protection and promotion of national cultures, in enabling cultural exchange. The bureaucracy writes and adheres to policy that suits its own ends, creating its own cultural platforms, and rarely seeking the opinion of "direct producers." Let's be frank with each other, in the cultural food chain, "direct producers" have become completely irrelevant. What's important is that cultural stuff happens, and that it is managed: Publishers are important, not writers; galleries and curators are important, not artists; literary festivals are important (events that prove something is happening), not the writers who participate.

Almost every European host country treats its transnational writers the same way it treats its immigrants. The civilized European milieu builds its immigrants residential neighborhoods, here and there making an effort to adapt the urban architecture to the hypothetical

tastes of future residents, discreet "orientalization" being a favorite.
Many stand in line to offer a warm welcome. Designers such as
the Dutch Cindy van den Bremen, for example, design their new
Muslim countrywomen modern hijabs—so they've got something
to wear when they play soccer, tennis, or take a dip at the pool.
The hosts do all kinds of things that they're ever so proud of, while
it never occurs to them that maybe they do so not to pull immigrants out of the ghetto, but rather to subtly keep them there, in
the ghetto of their identities and cultures, whatever either might
mean to them; to draw an invisible line between *us* and *them*, and
thus render many social spheres inaccessible. It is for this very same
reason that the publishing industry loves "exotic" authors, so long
as supply and demand are balanced. Many such authors fall over
themselves to ingratiate themselves with publishers—what else can
they do? And anyway, why wouldn't they?

Does transnational literature have its readers? And if it does, who
are they? Publishers have long since pandered to the hypothetical
tastes of the majority of consumers, and the majority's tastes will
inevitably reject many books as being culturally incomprehensible.
If the trend of "cultural comprehensibility"—the standardization of
literary taste—continues (and there's no reason why it won't), then
every conversation about transnational literature is but idle chatter
about a literary utopia. And anyway, how do we establish what is
authentic, and what is a product of market compromise? Our literary tastes, the tastes of literary consumers, have in time also become
standardized, self-adjusting to the products offered by the culture
industry. Let's not forget: The mass culture industry takes great care
in rearing its consumers. In this respect, transculturality has also
been transformed into a commercial trump card. In and of itself, the
term bears a positive inflection, but its incorporation in a literary

work needn't be any guarantee of literary quality, which is how it is
increasingly deployed in the literary marketplace. Today that marketplace offers a rich vein of such books, almost all well-regarded, and
their authors, protected by voguish theoretical terms—hybridity,
transnationality, transculturality, postcolonialism, ethnic and gender identities—take out the moral and aesthetic sweepstakes. Here,
literary kitsch is shaded by a smoke screen of ostensible political
correctness, heady cocktails mixing East and West, Amsterdam
Sufis and American housewives, Saharan Bedouins and Austrian
feminists, the burqa and Prada, the turban and Armani.

And where are my readers? Who's going to support me and my
little homespun enterprise? In the neoliberal system, of which literature is certainly part and parcel, my shop is doomed to close.
And what happens then (as I noted at the beginning) with my right
to defend my texts from the constraints of political, national, ethnic, and other ideological projections? My freedom has been eaten
by democracy—that's not actually a bad way to put it. There are,
in any case, any number of parks in which I can offer speeches to
the birds. What is the quality of a freedom where newspapers are
slowly disappearing because they're not able, so the claim goes, to
make a profit; when departments for many literatures are closing,
because there aren't any students (i.e., no profit!); when publishers unceremoniously dump their unprofitable writers, regardless of
whether those writers have won major international awards; when
the Greeks have to sell the family silver (one of Apollo's temples
in Athens is rumoured to be going under the hammer); when the
Dutch are fine with closing one of the oldest departments for astro-
physics in the world (in Utrecht), because it turns out that studying
the sun is unprofitable.

"Things are just a whisker better for you, because like it or not, at least you've got a kind of marketing angle. But me, I'm completely invisible, even within my own national literature," a Dutch writer friend of mine kvetches. And I mumble to myself, Christ, my *brand* really is a goodie—being "a Croatian writer who lives in Amsterdam" is just the sexiest thing ever. But I understand what my Amsterdam acquaintance is going on about. And really, how does one decide between two professional humiliations—between humiliating invisibility in one's "own" literary milieu, and humiliating visibility in a "foreign" one? The latter visibility inevitably based on details such as the incongruence between one's place of birth and one's place of residence, the color of one's skin, or an abandoned homeland that has just suffered a coup d'état. My Dutch acquaintance isn't far from the truth. Within the context of contemporary Dutch literature, or any other literature, where there is no longer any context; where there is no longer literature; where it is no longer of any importance whatsoever whether anyone reads books so long as they're buying them; where it is no longer of any importance whatsoever what people read, as long as they're reading; where the author is forced into the role of salesperson, promoter, and interpreter of his or her own work; only in such a deeply anti-literary and anti-intellectual context I am forced to feel lucky to be noticed as a "Croatian writer who lives in Amsterdam," and what's more, to be envied for it.

By now it should be obvious, the little pothole I overlooked when I abandoned my "national" literature is the sinkhole of the market. Times have certainly changed since I exited the "national" zone and entered my ON-zone. What was then a gesture of resistance is today barely understood by anyone. (Today, at least in Europe, recividist nationalisms and neo-fascisms are dismissed as temporary, isolated phenomena.) Of course, not all changes are immediately apparent: The cultural landscape remains the same, we're still surrounded by the things that were once and are still evidence of our raison d'être. We're still surrounded by bookshops, although in recent years we've noticed that the selection of books has petrified, that the same books by the same authors stand displayed in the same spots for years on end, as if bookshops are but a front, a camouflage for a parallel purpose. The officer in charge has done everything he should have, just forgetting to periodically swap the selection of books, make things look convincing. Libraries are still around too, although there are fewer of them: some shut with tears and a wail, others with a slam, and then there are those that refuse to go down without a fight, and so people organize petitions. Literary theorists, critics, the professoriate, readers, they're all still here, sure there aren't many of them, but still enough to make being a writer somewhat sensible. Publishers, editors, agents, they're all still in the room, though more and more often it occurs to us that they're not the same people anymore. It's as if no one really knows whether they're dead, or if it's we who are dead, just no one's gotten around to telling us. We've missed the boat on heaps of stuff. It's like we've turned up at a party, invitation safely in hand, but for some reason we have the dress code all wrong . . .

Literary life in the ON-zone seems to have lost any real sense. The ethical imperatives that once drove writers, intellectuals, and artists to "dispatriation" have in the meantime lost their value in the marketplace of ideas. The most frequent reasons for artistic and intellectual protest—fascism, nationalism, xenophobia, religious fundamentalism, political dictatorship, human rights violations, and the like—have been perverted by the voraciousness of the market, stripped of any ideological impetus and imbued with marketing clout, pathologizing even the most untainted "struggle for freedom," and transforming it into a struggle for commercial prestige.[4]

For this reason it's completely irrelevant whether tomorrow I leave my ON-zone and return "home," whether I set up shop somewhere else, or whether I stay where I am. For the first time I can see that my zone is just a ragged tent erected between the giant tower blocks of a new corporate culture. Although my books and the recognition they have received serve to confirm my professional status, they offer me no protection from the feeling that I've lost my "profession," not to mention my right to a "profession." I'm not alone, there are many like me. Many of us, without having noticed, have become home-less: for a quick buck, others, more powerful, have set the wrecking ball on our house.

Let's horse around for a moment—let's take the global success of E. L. James's *Fifty Shades of Grey* seriously (you can't *not* take those millions of copies sold seriously!), and baldly assert that the novel is the symbolic crown of today's corporate culture. And if we read the novel as exemplary of corporate culture—financial power as the only currency; the commutibility of the surrounding class of "oppressed" chauffeurs, secretaries and cooks who serve Christian and Anastasia; sadomasochism as the organizing principle of inter-personal relations in all domains, including sex; brutality, vulgarity,

---

4   In May 2013, the nationalist Croatian Democratic Union (HDZ) launched its election campaign wearing a new "party" dress. In place of the usual checker-board coat of arms, gingerbread hearts, circle dances, and similar down-home kitsch, these Croatian rednecks came out with minimalist posters bearing Jean Paul Sartre's "It is right to rebel!" slogan—poor old Sartre the ideological plume of Croatian conservatives!

violence, materialism; people being either masters or slaves—there's no chance of us missing a particular detail. At one point Christian gives Anastasia an "independent" (naturally!) publishing house as a little present. And thus, in this symbolic setting, my literary fate (and the fates of many of my brothers and sisters of the pen) depends entirely on the symbolic pairing of Anastasia and Christian. In this kind of setting, indentured by the principle of *publish or perish*, I belong to the servant class and can only count on employment as Anatasia and Christian's shoe-shine girl. And so it is my spit that softens their shoes, my tongue that licks them clean, my hair that makes them gleam.

Lamenting the death of the golden era of critical theory, Terry Eagleton memorably observes: "It seemed that God was not a structuralist." But it seems that God was not a writer either, certainly not a serious one. He slapped his bestseller together in seven days. And this all gets me thinking—if I've already bet my lot in life on literary values and lost—maybe I should bet my few remaining chips on their future. Because who knows, perhaps tomorrow, to my every flight of fancy, a translucent book, letters shimmering like plankton, will appear in the air before me; a liquid book into which I'll dive as if into a welcoming sea, surfacing with texts translucent and alive like a shoal of sardines. Perhaps tomorrow books will appear whose letters will converge in the air like swarms of gnats, with every stroke of my finger a coherent cluster of words forming . . . It's not so bad, I think, and imagine how in the very heart of defeat a new text is being born . . .

Dubravka Ugresic is a writer of novels (*Baba Yaga Laid an Egg, The Museum of Unconditional Surrender*), short story collections (*Lend Me Your Character, In the Jaws of Life*), and books of essays (*Nobody's Home, Karaoke Culture*). Born in the former Yugoslavia, Ugresic took a firm anti-nationalistic stand when war broke out in 1991, and was proclaimed a "traitor," a "public enemy," and a "witch." As a result, she left Croatia in 1993 and currently lives in Amsterdam. Her last collection of essays, *Karaoke Culture*, was a finalist for the National Book Critics Circle award for nonfiction.

D avid Williams is the author of *Writing Postcommunism: Towards a Literature of the East European Ruins*, which centers on the writings of Dubravka Ugresic. He is the translator of Ugresic's *Karaoke Culture* and Miljenko Jergović's *Mama Leone*, and is currently a DAAD postdoctoral fellow at the University of Konstanz.

Open Letter—the University of Rochester's nonprofit, literary translation press—is one of only a handful of publishing houses dedicated to increasing access to world literature for English readers. Publishing ten titles in translation each year, Open Letter searches for works that are extraordinary and influential, works that we hope will become the classics of tomorrow.

Making world literature available in English is crucial to opening our cultural borders, and its availability plays a vital role in maintaining a healthy and vibrant book culture. Open Letter strives to cultivate an audience for these works by helping readers discover imaginative, stunning works of fiction and poetry, and by creating a constellation of international writing that is engaging, stimulating, and enduring.

Current and forthcoming titles from Open Letter include works from Argentina, Bulgaria, Denmark, France, Germany, Italy, Latvia, Poland, Russia, and many other countries.

www.openletterbooks.org